# Cooperative Learning Grammar

Melissa Agnew
Stefanie McKoy

# Kagan

© 2012 by **Kagan Publishing**

This book is published by **Kagan Publishing**. All rights are reserved by **Kagan Publishing**. No part of this publication may be reproduced or transmitted in any form by any means, electronic or mechanical, including photocopy, recording, or any information storage and retrieval system, without prior written permission from **Kagan Publishing**. The blackline masters included in this book are intended for duplication only by classroom teachers who purchase the book, for use limited to their own classrooms. To obtain additional copies of this book, or information regarding professional development in cooperative learning or multiple intelligences, contact:

**Kagan Publishing**
981 Calle Amanecer
San Clemente, CA 92673
**1 (800) 933-2667**
www.KaganOnline.com

ISBN: 978-1-933445-11-3

# Cooperative Learning & Grammar
# TABLE OF CONTENTS

## STRUCTURES
- RallyCoach .................. 2
- Sage-N-Scribe ............. 4
- Quiz-Quiz-Trade ......... 6
- Find Someone Who ..... 8
- Fan-N-Pick ................. 10
- Showdown .................. 12
- Mix-N-Match .............. 14
- Find-N-Fix .................. 16

## Grammar Skills 1
## ANTONYMS, HOMOGRAPHS, HOMOPHONES, SYNONYMS
- Synonyms & Antonyms (RallyCoach/Sage-N-Scribe) .............. 20
- Synonyms & Antonyms (Showdown/Fan-N-Pick) .............. 21–23
- Homographs (Quiz-Quiz-Trade) .............. 24–31
- Homophones (Find-N-Fix) .............. 32
- Homophones (RallyCoach/Sage-N-Scribe) .............. 33
- Homographs (RallyCoach/Sage-N-Scribe) .............. 34
- Synonyms, Antonyms & Homophones (Find Someone Who) ... 35

## Grammar Skills 2
## PARTS OF SPEECH
- Verb Tense (Find Someone Who) .............. 38
- Verb Tense (Find-N-Fix) .............. 39
- Verb Usage (Showdown/Fan-N-Pick) .............. 40–42
- Helping Verbs (Find Someone Who) .............. 43
- Helping Verbs (Showdown/Fan-N-Pick) .............. 44–46
- Irregular Verbs (RallyCoach/Sage-N-Scribe) .............. 47
- Irregular Verbs (Find Someone Who) .............. 48
- Action Verbs (RallyCoach/Sage-N-Scribe) .............. 49
- Action or Being Verbs (Find Someone Who) .............. 50
- Comparative & Superlative Adjectives (RallyCoach/Sage-N-Scribe) .............. 51
- Descriptive Adjectives (Find Someone Who) .............. 52
- Adjectives (Showdown/Fan-N-Pick) .............. 53–55
- Adverbs (Rally Coach/Sage-N-Scribe) .............. 56
- Adverbs (Find Someone Who) .............. 57
- Adverbs (Showdown/Fan-N-Pick) .............. 58–60
- Nouns (RallyCoach/Sage-N-Scribe) .............. 61
- Nouns (Find Someone Who) .............. 62–63
- Common and Proper Nouns (Mix-N-Match) .............. 64–67
- Parts of Speech (RallyCoach/Sage-N-Scribe) .............. 68–69
- Parts of Speech (Find Someone Who) .............. 70
- Parts of Speech (Quiz-Quiz-Trade) .............. 71–77
- Plural Nouns: Adding -es and -s (RallyCoach/Sage-N-Scribe) .............. 78
- Plural Nouns: Adding -es and -s (Find Someone Who) .............. 79
- Plural Nouns: Words ending in -y (RallyCoach/Sage-N-Scribe) .............. 80
- Plural Nouns: Words ending in -y (Find Someone Who) .............. 81
- Plural Nouns: Words ending in -f or -fe (RallyCoach/Sage-N-Scribe) .. 82
- Plural Nouns: Words ending in -f or -fe (Find Someone Who) .............. 83
- Irregular Plural Nouns (RallyCoach/Sage-N-Scribe) .............. 84
- Irregular Plural Nouns (Find Someone Who) .............. 85

# Table of Contents

## Grammar Skills 2
### Parts of Speech (cont.)

- Plural Nouns: Review (Find-N-Fix) .................. 86
- Plural Nouns: Review (Find Someone Who) .................. 87
- Plural Nouns (Mix-N-Match) .................. 88–91
- Possessive Nouns (Find-N-Fix) .................. 92
- Possessive Nouns (RallyCoach/Sage-N-Scribe) .................. 93
- Possessive Nouns (Find Someone Who) .................. 94
- Possessive Nouns (Quiz-Quiz-Trade) .................. 95–102
- Possessive Pronouns (Find Someone Who) .................. 103
- Pronouns (RallyCoach/Sage-N-Scribe) .................. 104
- Pronouns (Showdown/Fan-N-Pick) .................. 105–107
- Pronouns (Quiz-Quiz-Trade) .................. 108–114
- Suffixes (RallyCoach/Sage-N-Scribe) .................. 115
- Suffixes & Prefixes (Find Someone Who) .................. 116–117
- Prefix, Suffix & Root words (Quiz-Quiz-Trade) .................. 118–125
- Articles (Find-N-Fix) .................. 126
- Articles (RallyCoach/Sage-N-Scribe) .................. 127
- Compound Words (RallyCoach/Sage-N-Scribe) .................. 128
- Compound Words (Find Someone Who) .................. 129
- Compound Words (Mix-N-Match) .................. 130–133
- Contractions (Find-N-Fix) .................. 134
- Contractions (RallyCoach/Sage-N-Scribe) .................. 135–138
- Contractions (Find Someone Who) .................. 139–140
- Contractions (Quiz-Quiz-Trade) .................. 141–156
- Prepositions (RallyCoach/Sage-N-Scribe) .................. 157

## Grammar Skills 3
### Punctuation

- Capital Letters (Find-N-Fix) .................. 160
- Capital Letters (RallyCoach/Sage-N-Scribe) .................. 161–162
- Capital Letters (Find Someone Who) .................. 163
- Capital Letters (Showdown/Fan-N-Pick) .................. 164–166
- Capitalization of Proper Nouns (RallyCoach/Sage-N-Scribe) .................. 167
- Capital Letters (Mix-N-Match) .................. 168–171
- Commas (Find-N-Fix) .................. 172
- Commas in a Series, Dates & Locations (RallyCoach/Sage-N-Scribe) .................. 173–174
- Commas (Find Someone Who) .................. 175
- Punctuation (Find-N-Fix) .................. 176
- Punctuation (Find Someone Who) .................. 177–179
- Punctuation (Mix-N-Match) .................. 180–183
- Using Quotation Marks (RallyCoach/Sage-N-Scribe) .................. 184
- Quotation Marks & Punctuation (Find Someone Who) .................. 185
- Quotation Marks (Quiz-Quiz-Trade) .................. 186–191
- Capital Letters & Punctuation (RallyCoach/Sage-N-Scribe) .................. 192–193
- Capital Letters & Punctuation (Find Someone Who) .................. 194–195
- Capitalization & Punctuation (Quiz-Quiz-Trade) .................. 196–203

# TABLE OF CONTENTS

## Grammar Skills 4
## SENTENCES

- Simple Subject
  (RallyCoach/Sage-N-Scribe) .............. 206
- Simple Subject
  (Find Someone Who) ........................ 207
- Simple Predicate
  (RallyCoach/Sage-N-Scribe) .............. 208
- Simple Predicate
  (Find Someone Who) ........................ 209
- Complete Subject
  (RallyCoach/Sage-N-Scribe) .............. 210
- Complete Subject
  (Find Someone Who) ........................ 211
- Complete Predicate
  (RallyCoach/Sage-N-Scribe) .............. 212
- Complete Predicate
  (Find Someone Who) ........................ 213
- Subject & Predicate
  (RallyCoach/Sage-N-Scribe) .............. 214
- Complete Subject & Predicate
  (RallyCoach/Sage-N-Scribe) .............. 215
- Subject & Predicate
  (Find Someone Who) ........................ 216
- Complete Subject & Predicate
  (Quiz-Quiz-Trade) ..................... 217–224
- Complete Sentences
  (Find-N-Fix) ................................... 225
- Dependent & Independent Clauses
  (Find Someone Who) ........................ 226
- Independent Clauses & Conjunctions
  (RallyCoach/Sage-N-Scribe) .............. 227
- Complete Sentences
  (Showdown/Fan-N-Pick) ........... 228–230
- Combining Sentences
  (RallyCoach/Sage-N-Scribe) .............. 231
- Declarative & Imperative Sentences
  (RallyCoach/Sage-N-Scribe) .............. 232
- Interrogative & Exclamatory Sentences
  (RallyCoach/Sage-N-Scribe) .............. 233
- Types of Sentences
  (RallyCoach/Sage-N-Scribe) ..... 234–235
- Types of Sentences
  (Find Someone Who) ........................ 236

## ANSWER KEY

- Antonyms, Homographs, Homophones, Synonyms
  (Grammar Skills 1) .............................. 238
- Parts of Speech
  (Grammar Skills 2) ...................... 239-246
- Punctuation
  (Grammar Skills 3) ..................... 247–250
- Sentences (Grammar Skills 4) ... 251–255

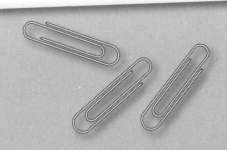

Cooperative Learning & Grammar
Kagan Publishing • 1 (800) 933-2667 • www.KaganOnline.com

# About the Authors

Melissa Agnew graduated from Missouri State University in Springfield, Missouri, with a Bachelor of Arts degree in Elementary Education and a Master of Arts degree in Educational Administration. She has taught third grade for seven years in the Branson School District. In those seven years, she received her eMINTS certification and served as both team leader and curriculum leader. In addition, Melissa has also worked with groups of English Language Learners and Gifted Student Clusters in her regular education classroom. She resides in Springfield, Missouri, with her husband of two years and their young son. She enjoys cooking, going to the gym, and taking care of her family.

Stefanie McKoy graduated from Missouri State University in Springfield, Missouri, with a Bachelor of Arts degree in Elementary Education and earned a Master of Arts degree in Educational Technology Leadership from the University of Arkansas in Fayetteville. She is currently certified in both Early Childhood and Elementary Education, and has her eMINTS certification. Stefanie teaches third grade at Branson School District. She has served on her school's communication arts committee and was coordinator for the after-school tutoring program serving four grade levels and over 100 students. This past year she has been co-teaching with the special education department serving eight learning disabled students in her regular education classroom. Stefanie resides in Ozark, Missouri, with her husband of three years and their young son. She enjoys reading, building Web sites, and drinking coffee.

## Thank You

Thanks go to Laurie Kagan and Miguel Kagan, for the feedback and for the opportunity to share this book with others; Jeremie Rujanawech for making the book come alive with his design; Becky Herrington for managing the publication; Alex Core for cover design and color; Erin Kant for illustrations, and Kim Fields for copyediting.

We would like to thank James Larimore from Branson Photography for taking our pictures for the book.

# Introduction

Dear Educator,

Thank you for taking interest in *Cooperative Learning & Grammar*. We have worked very hard to bring you the best activities to use in the classroom. As current educators ourselves, we saw a need to have more activities on hand. If you are like us, you'll find using Kagan Cooperative Structures will greatly improve classroom learning. We were continually creating worksheets and activities to use in the classroom, and since we found ourselves using our activities numerous times and other teachers were coming to us for our creations, we decided to compile it all into a book to share with you!

The structures you will most commonly find in this book include Find Someone Who, RallyCoach or Sage-N-Scribe, and Find-N-Fix. We know that teachers are still often held to collecting grades and showing student learning through "worksheet" activities. We tried to provide you with several activities for each content standard utilizing different structures. We also tried to provide scaffolding activities to increase understanding during lessons. We included a few Quiz-Quiz-Trade, Fan-N-Pick or Showdown, and Mix-N-Match activities as we know these are some of our students' favorites.

During the process of creating this book, we had overwhelming encouragement and assistance from our friends at Branson Elementary West in Branson, Missouri. We could not have done it without all the uplifting e-mails and willingness to try out our activities in the classroom. We also thank our principal, Mike Dawson, for being understanding of our new endeavor and always providing any support we might need. We must also thank our students who were our mini-editors and testers! They were never afraid to share their opinions.

In addition we would like to extend a huge thank-you to our families for the continuous support and understanding as we worked on our activities. We couldn't have done it without you!

So, we leave you with our collection of grammar activities for grades 3-5. Enjoy the fun your students will have while learning in your classroom!

Your partners in education,
Melissa Agnew and Stefanie McKoy

# STRUCTURES

**Structure 1**
RallyCoach .................. 2

**Structure 2**
Sage-N-Scribe .................. 4

**Structure 3**
Quiz-Quiz-Trade .................. 6

**Structure 4**
Find Someone Who ....... 8

**Structure 5**
Fan-N-Pick .................. 10

**Structure 6**
Showdown .................. 12

**Structure 7**
Mix-N-Match .................. 14

**Structure 8**
Find-N-Fix .................. 16

# Structure 1
# RallyCoach

*Partners take turns, one solving a problem while the other coaches.*

**Setup:** The teacher prepares a set of problems. Each pair receives the problem worksheet or a piece of paper to answer the problems and one pencil or pen.

**1. Partner A Solves**
In shoulder partners, Partner A solves the first problem, talking about his or her thinking.

**2. Partner B Coaches**
Partner B acts as the coach. Partner B watches, listens, and checks. If Partner A gets an incorrect answer or needs help, Partner B coaches. If Partner A solves the problem correctly, Partner B praises.

**3. Partner B Solves**
Students switch roles and Partner B now solves the problem, talking about it.

**4. Partner A Coaches**
Partner A now acts as the coach: watching, listening, checking, coaching, and praising.

**5. Continue Solving**
The process is repeated for each new problem.

## Variations

- **RallyCoach for Oral Problems.** *The teacher gives the class problems orally, and students use RallyCoach to solve the problems.*

# RallyCoach Activities

## Grammar Skills 1
### Antonyms, Homographs, Homophones, Synonyms
- Synonyms & Antonyms ........................ 20
- Homophones ...................................... 33
- Homographs ...................................... 34

## Grammar Skills 2
### Parts of Speech
- Irregular Verbs ................................... 47
- Action Verbs ...................................... 49
- Comparative & Superlative Adjectives .. 51
- Adverbs ............................................. 56
- Nouns ................................................ 61
- Parts of Speech ............................. 68–69
- Plural Nouns: Adding -es and -s ......... 78
- Plural Nouns: Words ending in -y ........ 80
- Plural Nouns: Words ending in -f or -fe ..................................... 82
- Irregular Plural Nouns ........................ 84
- Possessive Nouns .............................. 93
- Pronouns ......................................... 104
- Suffixes ........................................... 115
- Articles ............................................ 127
- Compound Words ............................ 128
- Contractions .............................. 135–138
- Prepositions .................................... 157

## Grammar Skills 3
### Punctuation
- Capital Letters .......................... 161–162
- Capitalization of Proper Nouns ........... 167
- Commas in a Series, Dates & Locations ...................... 173–174
- Using Quotation Marks ..................... 184
- Capital Letters & Punctuation ...... 192–193

## Grammar Skills 4
### Sentences
- Simple Subject .................................. 206
- Simple Predicate .............................. 208
- Complete Subject ............................. 210
- Complete Predicate .......................... 212
- Subject & Predicate .......................... 214
- Complete Subject & Predicate ........... 215
- Independent Clauses & Conjunctions ............................... 227
- Combining Sentences ....................... 231
- Declarative & Imperative Sentences ... 232
- Interrogative & Exclamatory Sentences ................... 233
- Types of Sentences .................... 234–235

*Cooperative Learning & Grammar*

# Structure 2
# SAGE-N-SCRIBE

*Partners take turns being the Sage and Scribe.*

**Setup:** In pairs, Student A is the Sage; Student B is the Scribe. Each pair is given a set of problems to solve, half for each partner. Partners can share a pencil or pen.

**1. Sage Instructs Scribe**
The Sage orally instructs the Scribe how to perform a task or solve a problem. For example, the Sage's instructions to the Scribe for correcting sentences for grammar might sound like this: *"To fix this sentence, first capitalize the proper noun in the sentence."*

**2. Scribe Writes Solution, Tutors if Necessary**
The Scribe solves the problem in writing according to the Sage's step-by-step oral instructions. If the Sage gives incorrect instructions, the Scribe tutors the Sage. *"I don't think that's correct. I think..."*

**3. Scribe Praises Sage**
After completion of the problem, the Scribe praises the Sage. *"You aced that one!"*

**4. Partners Switch Roles**
Students switch roles for the next problem or task.

## Hints

- **Polite Tutoring.** Sometimes the Sage will make errors in their instructions. Teach the class how to politely tell their partners that they missed a step or made an error. Reinforce that the point is not to see who is smarter or to see who can make the fewest errors. The goal is for everyone to work together and for everyone to learn.

- **Checkpoint.** Have a place in the room where students can go to check answers if both partners are stuck.

# Sage-N-Scribe Activities

### Grammar Skills 1
## Antonyms, Homographs, Homophones, Synonyms
- Synonyms & Antonyms .................... 20
- Homophones ................................... 33
- Homographs ..................................... 34

### Grammar Skills 2
## Parts of Speech
- Irregular Verbs ................................ 47
- Action Verbs .................................... 49
- Comparative & Superlative Adjectives .. 51
- Adverbs ........................................... 56
- Nouns .............................................. 61
- Parts of Speech ......................... 68–69
- Plural Nouns: Adding -es and -s ....... 78
- Plural Nouns: Words ending in -y ......... 80
- Plural Nouns: Words ending in -f or -fe ................................. 82
- Irregular Plural Nouns ..................... 84
- Possessive Nouns ............................ 93
- Pronouns ....................................... 104
- Suffixes .......................................... 115
- Articles ........................................... 127
- Compound Words .......................... 128
- Contractions ........................... 135–138
- Prepositions .................................. 157

### Grammar Skills 3
## Punctuation
- Capital Letters ........................ 161–162
- Capitalization of Proper Nouns ........... 167
- Commas in a Series, Dates & Locations ................... 173–174
- Using Quotation Marks ................... 184
- Capital Letters & Punctuation ...... 192–193

### Grammar Skills 4
## Sentences
- Simple Subject ............................... 206
- Simple Predicate ............................ 208
- Complete Subject ........................... 210
- Complete Predicate ........................ 212
- Subject & Predicate ........................ 214
- Complete Subject & Predicate ........... 215
- Independent Clauses & Conjunctions .............................. 227
- Combining Sentences .................... 231
- Declarative & Imperative Sentences ... 232
- Interrogative & Exclamatory Sentences ................. 233
- Types of Sentences ................ 234–235

## Structure 3
# Quiz-Quiz-Trade

Students quiz a partner, get quizzed by a partner, and then trade cards to repeat the process with a new partner.

**Setup:** The teacher provides or students create cards, each with a grammar problem.

**1. Students Pair Up**
With a card in one hand and the other hand raised, each student stands up, puts a hand up, and pairs up with a classmate. They give each other a high five as they pair up. *"Alright everyone, stand up, hand up, pair up. High five when you pair up and lower your hands so everyone can quickly find a partner with a hand up."*

**2. Partner A Quizzes**
In the pair, Partner A asks Partner B a question relating to his or her card. For example, *"My card says* Hasn't. Hasn't *is a contraction for what two words?"*

**3. Partner B Answers**
Partner B answers Partner A's question: *"Has not."*

**4. Partner A Praises or Coaches**
If Partner B answers correctly, Partner A praises him or her. If Partner B answers incorrectly, Partner A provides the correct answer and coaches or tutors Partner B.

**5. Switch Roles**
Partners switch roles. Partner B now asks the question and offers praise or coaches.

**6. Partners Trade Cards**
Before departing and looking for new partners, partners trade cards. This way, students have a new card for each new pairing.

**7. Continue Quizzing and Trading**
Partners split up and continue quizzing and getting quizzed by new partners. When done, they trade cards again and find a new partner.

# Quiz-Quiz-Trade Activities

### Grammar Skills 1
## Antonyms, Homographs, Homophones, Synonyms
- Homographs .................................. 24–31

### Grammar Skills 2
## Parts of Speech
- Parts of Speech ................................. 71–77
- Possessive Nouns ........................ 95–102
- Pronouns ..................................... 108–114
- Prefix, Suffix & Root Words .......... 118–125
- Contractions ................................. 141–156

### Grammar Skills 3
## Punctuation
- Quotation Marks ......................... 186–191
- Capitalization & Punctuation ....... 196–203

### Grammar Skills 4
## Sentences
- Complete Subject & Predicate .... 217–224

## Structure 4
# Find Someone Who

Students circulate through the classroom, forming and reforming pairs, trying to "find someone who" knows an answer, then they become "someone who knows."

**Setup:** The teacher prepares a worksheet or questions for students.

**1. Students Mix**
With worksheets in one hand and the other hand raised, students circulate through the room until they find a partner. *"Mix in the room and pair up with a student with a hand up. Put your hands down and ask each other one question from your sheet. If your partner knows an answer, write the answer in your own words, then have your partner sign your sheet to show he or she agrees."*

**2. Partner A Asks Question**
In pairs, Partner A asks a question from the worksheet; Partner B responds. Partner A records the answer on his or her own worksheet.

**3. Partner B Checks**
Partner B checks the answer and initials it that he or she agrees.

**4. Partner B Asks Question**
Partner B now asks a question; Partner A responds. Partner B records the answer on his or her own worksheet.

**5. Partner A Checks**
Partner A checks the answer and initials it that he or she agrees.

**6. Partners Depart**
Partners shake hands, part, and raise a hand again as they search for a new partner.

**7. Continue Finding Someone Who**
Students continue mixing and pairing until their worksheets are complete.

**8. Students Sit**
When their worksheets are completed, students sit down; seated students may be approached by others as a resource.

**9. Teams Compare Answers**
When all students are done, or the teacher calls time, students return to their teams to compare answers; if there is disagreement or uncertainty, they can consult a neighbor team or raise four hands to ask a team question. *"Please return to your team and RoundRobin read the question and share the answer. If you have different answers, work it out in your team. If you can't agree, get help from a nearby team, or ask a team question."*

### Variations

- **Info Search.** Start with a topic on which all students have no information. Every student gets an Info Search form which is a worksheet with questions on it. If there are ten questions on the worksheet, ten students get an answer sheet with one answer filled in. Students then play the game just like Find-Someone-Who. Soon all students have all the answers.

- **Find-Those-Who.** Students circulate about the classroom in pairs or teams searching for another pair or team that has the answers.

# Find Someone Who ACTIVITIES

## Grammar Skills 1
### ANTONYMS, HOMOGRAPHS, HOMOPHONES, SYNONYMS

- Synonyms, Antonyms & Homonyms ..................................35

## Grammar Skills 2
### PARTS OF SPEECH

- Verb Tense ..................................38
- Helping Verbs ............................43
- Irregular Verbs ..........................48
- Action or Being Verbs ................50
- Descriptive Adjectives ................52
- Adverbs .....................................57
- Nouns ................................. 62–63
- Parts of Speech .........................70
- Plural Nouns: Adding -es and -s ..........79
- Plural Nouns: Words ending in -y ......... 81
- Plural Nouns: Words ending in -f or -fe .............................. 83
- Irregular Plural Nouns .................85
- Plural Nouns: Review ..................87
- Possessive Nouns .......................94
- Possessive Pronouns ................. 103
- Suffixes & Prefixes ............. 116–117
- Compound Words ..................... 129
- Contractions ..................... 139–140

## Grammar Skills 3
### PUNCTUATION

- Capital Letters ......................... 163
- Commas ................................... 175
- Punctuation ..................... 177–179
- Quotation Marks & Punctuation ......... 185
- Capital Letters & Punctuation ....... 194–195

## Grammar Skills 4
### SENTENCES

- Simple Subject .........................207
- Simple Predicate .......................209
- Complete Subject ..................... 211
- Complete Predicate ................... 213
- Subject and Predicate ................ 216
- Dependent & Independent Clauses ..226
- Types of Sentences ...................236

## Structure 5
# Fan-N-Pick

Teammates play a card game to respond to questions. Roles rotate with each new question.

**Setup:** Each team receives a set of question or problem cards.

**1. Student #1 Fans Cards**
Student #1 holds the question cards in a fan and says, *"Pick a card, any card!"*

**2. Student #2 Picks a Card**
Student #2 picks a card, reads the question aloud, and allows five seconds of think time. *"Which word is the verb in the following sentence? 'Sue kicked the ball.'"*

**3. Student #3 Answers**
Student #3 answers the question. *"The verb is 'kicked.'"*

**4. Student #4 Responds**
Student #4 responds to the answer.
- For right or wrong answers: Student #4 checks the answer and then either praises or tutors the student who answered. *"That's correct! You're a true genius."* or *"I don't think that's correct; let's solve it again together."*
- For higher-level thinking questions that have no right or wrong answer: Student #4 does not check for correctness, but praises and paraphrases the thinking that went into the answer. *"Excellent response. I like the way you approached the question."*

**5. Rotate Roles**
Teammates rotate roles, one person clockwise for each new round.

## Variations

- **Fan-N-Spin.** The team plays Fan-N-Pick with a random team selector spinner. After the question is read, the reader spins the spinner and the selected student answers. This keeps everyone thinking because anyone may be called on to answer at any point.

- **Pair Fan-N-Pick.** Fan-N-Pick can be played in pairs. Student #1 fans the question cards. Student #2 picks and reads a question card. Student #1 answers. Student #2 tutors or praises. Students switch roles for each new question.

# Fan-N-Pick Activities

### Grammar Skills 1
## ANTONYMS, HOMOGRAPHS, HOMOPHONES, SYNONYMS
- Synonyms & Antonyms .................. 21–23

### Grammar Skills 2
## PARTS OF SPEECH
- Verb Usage ..................... 40–42
- Helping Verbs ................. 44–46
- Adjectives ....................... 53–55
- Adverbs ............................. 58–60
- Pronouns ........................ 105–107

### Grammar Skills 3
## PUNCTUATION
- Capital Letters ............................. 164–166

### Grammar Skills 4
## SENTENCES
- Complete Sentences ................. 228–230

## Structure 6
# SHOWDOWN

*When the Showdown Captain calls, "Showdown!" teammates all display their own answers. Teammates either celebrate or tutor, and then celebrate.*

**Setup:** The teacher prepares questions or problems. Questions may be provided to each team as question cards that they stack facedown in the center of the table. Each student has a slate or a response board and a writing utensil.

**1. Teacher Selects Showdown Captain**
The teacher selects one student on each team to be the Showdown Captain for the first round. *"Student #4 is the first Showdown captain. Rotate the role clockwise after each question."*

**2. Showdown Captain Reads Question**
The Showdown Captain reads the first question. If using question cards, the Showdown Captain draws the top card, reads the question, and provides think time. *"Think about your answer, then write it down."*

**3. Students Answer Independently**
Working alone, all students write their answers.

**4. Teammates Signal When Done**
When finished, teammates signal they're ready by turning over their response boards, putting down their markers, or giving a hand signal.

**5. Showdown Captain calls, "Showdown"**
The Showdown Captain calls, *"Showdown!"*

**6. Teams Show Answers**
Teammates show their answers and RoundRobin state them in turn.

**7. Teams Check for Accuracy**
The Showdown Captain leads the team in checking for accuracy. *"Great. We all got the same answer."*

**8. Celebrate or Coach**
If the all teammates have the correct answer, the team celebrates; if not, teammates coach the student or students with the incorrect answer, then celebrate.

**9. Rotate Captain Role**
The person on the left of the Showdown Captain becomes the Showdown Captain for the next round.

*Modifications:*
*Rather than cards, students can play Showdown with oral questions from the teacher, or from questions on a handout or questions displayed by a projector.*

### Variation

- **Team Showdown.** *Each team works on the same problem. When all teams have an answer, they show their team slate and compare answers with other teams. If a team misses a problem, instruction from another team or the teacher may be needed.*

# Showdown Activities

### Grammar Skills 1
## ANTONYMS, HOMOGRAPHS, HOMOPHONES, SYNONYMS
- Synonyms & Antonyms .................. 21–23

### Grammar Skills 2
## PARTS OF SPEECH
- Verb Usage ..................................... 40–42
- Helping Verbs ............................... 44–46
- Adjectives ...................................... 53–55
- Adverbs ........................................... 58–60
- Pronouns ........................................ 105–107

### Grammar Skills 3
## PUNCTUATION
- Capital Letters ............................. 164–166

### Grammar Skills 4
## SENTENCES
- Complete Sentences ................... 228–230

# Structure 7
# Mix-N-Match

Students mix, repeatedly quizzing new partners and trading cards. Afterward, they rush to find a partner with the card that matches theirs.

**Setup:** The teacher provides, or students create, pairs of matching cards.

**1. Students Mix and Pair**
With a card in one hand and the other hand raised, each student mixes around the room, looking for a partner with a raised hand. When they pair up, they give each other a high five. *"Pair up with another student with a raised hand. Give each other a high five and lower your hands."*

**2. Partner A Asks Question**
In the pair, Partner A asks the other a question relating to his or her card. For example, *"What type of sentence ends with this punctuation mark?"*

**3. Partner B Answers**
Partner B answers Partner A's question. *"If it ends with an exclamation mark, it's an exclamatory sentence."*

**4. Partner A Praises or Coaches**
If Partner B answers correctly, Partner A praises him or her. *"That's right. Great grammar skills."* If Partner B answers incorrectly, Partner A provides the correct answer and coaches or tutors Partner B. *"I don't think that's correct. Let's look at it again."*

**5. Switch Roles**
Partners switch roles. Partner B now asks the question and offers praise or coaches.

**6. Partners Trade Cards**
Before departing and looking for new partners, partners trade cards. This way, students have a new card for each new pairing.

**7. Continue Quizzing and Trading**
Partners split up and continue quizzing and getting quizzed by new partners. When done, they trade cards again and find a new partner.

**8. Teacher Calls "Freeze"**
After a sufficient time of quizzing and trading cards, the teacher calls, *"Freeze."* Students freeze, hide their cards, and think of their match.

**9. Find Match**
The teacher calls, *"Match."* Students search for a classmate with the matching card. When they find each other, they move to the outside of the classroom so students still searching for a match can find each other more easily.

*Optional:*
Teacher may post a class graph to record the time it takes for students to find their matching partners. Students try to beat their class record.

# Mix-N-Match Activities

### Grammar Skills 2
# PARTS OF SPEECH
- Common & Proper Nouns ............... 64–67
- Plural Nouns ................................. 88–91
- Compound Words ....................... 130–133

### Grammar Skills 3
# PUNCTUATION
- Capital Letters ............................ 168–171
- Punctuation ................................ 180–183

## Structure 8
# Find-N-Fix

*Teammates find which answer is incorrect, then fix it.*

**Setup:** Each teammate receives a Find-N-Fix worksheet and a set of Find-N-Fix Cards.

**1. Select a Captain**
One student on each team is selected as the Captain. The Captain's role is to lead the team through one problem.

**2. Captain Reads Problem**
The Captain reads the first set of problems and asks the team which has an incorrect answer. For example, there may be three sentences, one with incorrect punctuation.

**3. Students Pick Cards**
Each teammate picks one of the three Find-N-Fix Cards and holds it to his or her chin so teammates can't see which card he or she chose. For example, a teammate thinks the second sentence is missing commas, so she selects the card, "#2 needs to be fixed."

**4. Reveal Cards**
When all teammates have their cards to the their chins, the Captain says, "Reveal your answer." Students show their answers.

**5. Celebrate or Coach**
If all teammates have the same answer, they celebrate with a quick team cheer or handshake. Teammates coach the student(s) with the incorrect answer.

**6. Teammates Correct Worksheets**
Each teammate circles the incorrect answer on his or her worksheet and fixes the answer so it is correct. If necessary, students may receive help from teammates.

**7. Rotate Captain Role**
The Captain role is rotated one student clockwise for each new problem.

**8. Continue Playing**
Students continue playing until they complete the worksheet or until time is up.

Page 18

### Variations

- **Pair Find-N-Fix.** Students play Find-N-Fix in pairs. Partners take turns being the Captain for each set of problems.

- **Shared Find-N-Fix Worksheets.** Teams or pairs can share a worksheet. In this case, it is the Captain's job to fix the problem on the worksheet, yet the Captain must first receive consensus from teammates (or partner) before making the correction.

# Find-N-Fix Activities

### Grammar Skills 1
## Antonyms, Homographs, Homophones, Synonyms
- Homophones..........................32

### Grammar Skills 2
## Parts of Speech
- Verb Tense.................................39
- Plural Nouns: Review ...................86
- Possessive Nouns .........................92
- Articles........................................126
- Contractions................................134

### Grammar Skills 3
## Punctuation
- Capital Letters ........................ 160
- Commas ................................. 172
- Punctuation............................ 176

### Grammar Skills 4
## Sentences
- Complete Sentences ...................225

# Find-N-Fix Response Cards

**Directions:** Cut out cards along the dotted line. In teams, hold up response cards indicating which answer needs to be fixed.

## #1 needs to be fixed

## #2 needs to be fixed

## #3 needs to be fixed

## Grammar Skills 1
# Antonyms, Homographs, Homophones, Synonyms

- **Synonyms & Antonyms**
  (RallyCoach/Sage-N-Scribe) .......................... 20
- **Synonyms & Antonyms**
  (Showdown/Fan-N-Pick) ........................ 21–23
- **Homographs** (Quiz-Quiz-Trade) .............. 24–31
- **Homophones** (Find-N-Fix) .......................... 32
- **Homophones**
  (RallyCoach/Sage-N-Scribe) .......................... 33
- **Homographs**
  (RallyCoach/Sage-N-Scribe) .......................... 34
- **Synonyms, Antonyms & Homonyms**
  (Find Someone Who) ..................................... 35

- **Answer Key** ................................................... 238

# Synonyms & Antonyms
## RallyCoach/Sage-N-Scribe

**Instructions:** For each problem, decide if the word pairs are synonyms or antonyms. Take turns working with your partner to solve the problems using RallyCoach or Sage-N-Scribe.

### Partner A

Name _____

1. accept — refuse
2. dare — challenge
3. succeed — fail
4. argument — dispute
5. permanent — temporary
6. simple — complicated
7. impatient — anxious
8. majority — minority

### Partner B

Name _____

1. join — separate
2. poverty — wealth
3. increase — decrease
4. estimate — guess
5. offer — proposal
6. innocent — guilty
7. blend — combine
8. borrow — lend

# Synonyms & Antonyms
## Showdown/Fan-N-Pick

**Instructions:** Copy one set of cards for each team. Cut out each card along the dotted line. Give each team a set of cards to play Fan-N-Pick or Showdown.

### Synonyms & Antonyms

**1.** Which word pair below are antonyms?
- a. high – low
- b. dainty – fragile
- c. small – little

**2.** Which word pair below are synonyms?
- a. day – night
- b. boy – girl
- c. sofa – couch

**3.** Which word pair below are synonyms?
- a. clean – dirty
- b. night – evening
- c. alive – dead

**4.** Which word pair below are synonyms?
- a. smart – intelligent
- b. black – white
- c. up – down

**5.** Which word pair below are antonyms?
- a. cry – weep
- b. fat – skinny
- c. car – automobile

**6.** Which word pair below are antonyms?
- a. pretty – beautiful
- b. ill – sick
- c. tall – short

*Cooperative Learning & Grammar*
Kagan Publishing • 1 (800) 933-2667 • www.KaganOnline.com

Antonyms, Homographs, Homophones, Synonyms

# SYNONYMS & ANTONYMS
## Showdown/Fan-N-Pick

**Instructions:** Copy one set of cards for each team. Cut out each card along the dotted line. Give each team a set of cards to play Fan-N-Pick or Showdown.

---

**SYNONYMS & ANTONYMS**

**7.** Which antonym could take the place of the underlined word in the sentence below?

The small <u>infant</u> was crying because it was hungry.

- a. adult
- b. baby
- c. human

---

**SYNONYMS & ANTONYMS**

**8.** Which synonym could take the place of the underlined word in the sentence below?

Sara had on a <u>beautiful</u> dress.

- a. ugly
- b. pretty
- c. long

---

**SYNONYMS & ANTONYMS**

**9.** Which synonym could take the place of the underlined word in the sentence below?

The principal wanted to have a <u>talk</u> with my parents.

- a. chat
- b. yell
- c. brief

---

**SYNONYMS & ANTONYMS**

**10.** Which synonym could take the place of the underlined word in the sentence below?

My dad had to <u>fix</u> the chain on my bike.

- a. break
- b. pay
- c. repair

---

**SYNONYMS & ANTONYMS**

**11.** Which antonym could take the place of the underlined word in the sentence below?

My mom keeps the snacks on a <u>high</u> shelf in the pantry.

- a. tall
- b. low
- c. long

---

**SYNONYMS & ANTONYMS**

**12.** Which antonym could take the place of the underlined word in the sentence below?

The <u>old</u> man had a large bag of groceries.

- a. young
- b. elderly
- c. grey

# Synonyms & Antonyms
## Showdown/Fan-N-Pick

**Instructions:** Copy one set of cards for each team. Cut out each card along the dotted line. Give each team a set of cards to play Fan-N-Pick or Showdown.

---

**Synonyms & Antonyms**

**13.** Which antonym could take the place of the underlined word in the sentence below?

I must check <u>out</u> the book at the library.

a. from
b. away
c. in

---

**Synonyms & Antonyms**

**14.** Which word pair below are antonyms?

a. open – closed
b. angry – mad
c. funny – silly

---

**Synonyms & Antonyms**

**15.** Which synonym could take the place of the underlined word in the sentence below?

That movie made me <u>cry</u>.

a. mad
b. weep
c. sick

---

**Synonyms & Antonyms**

**16.** Which word pair below are synonyms?

a. fast – slow
b. laugh – giggle
c. begin – end

---

**Synonyms & Antonyms**

**17.** Which antonym could take the place of the underlined word in the sentence below?

My brother's car goes really <u>fast</u>.

a. speedy
b. slow
c. fancy

---

**Synonyms & Antonyms**

**18.** Which word pair below are antonyms?

a. bugs – insects
b. giggle – cry
c. damp – wet

# HOMOGRAPHS
## Quiz-Quiz-Trade

**Instructions:** Cut out each card along the dotted line. Then fold each card in half so the question is on one side and the answer is on the back. Glue or tape the cards together to keep the answers and questions on opposite sides.

### 1 — HOMOGRAPHS Question

Which word best completes both sentences below?

The ____ flew into the cave.

John was missing his baseball ____.

a. bat
b. ball
c. glove

### 1 — HOMOGRAPHS Answer

**a. bat**

### 2 — HOMOGRAPHS Question

Which word best completes both sentences below?

There was a dirty _____ around the tub.

Sophia's mom gave her a silver _____.

a. mark
b. bracelet
c. ring

### 2 — HOMOGRAPHS Answer

**c. ring**

### 3 — HOMOGRAPHS Question

Which word best completes both sentences below?

The kids will get to _____ for another hour.

We went to see a _____ at the theater.

a. movie
b. play
c. run

### 3 — HOMOGRAPHS Answer

**b. play**

24 — Antonyms, Homographs, Homophones, Synonyms

*Cooperative Learning & Grammar*
Kagan Publishing • 1 (800) 933-2667 • www.KaganOnline.com

# HOMOGRAPHS
## Quiz-Quiz-Trade

**Instructions:** Cut out each card along the dotted line. Then fold each card in half so the question is on one side and the answer is on the back. Glue or tape the cards together to keep the answers and questions on opposite sides.

**4** — HOMOGRAPHS Question

Which word best completes both sentences below?

Sam didn't feel ____ today.

Our neighbors are digging a new ____.

a. well
b. sick
c. hole

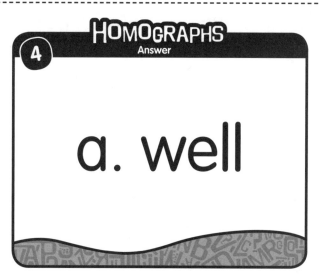

**4** — HOMOGRAPHS Answer

a. well

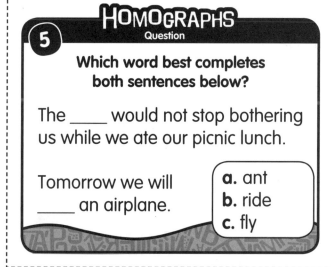

**5** — HOMOGRAPHS Question

Which word best completes both sentences below?

The ____ would not stop bothering us while we ate our picnic lunch.

Tomorrow we will ____ an airplane.

a. ant
b. ride
c. fly

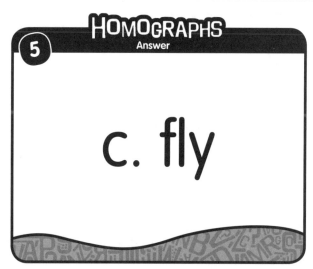

**5** — HOMOGRAPHS Answer

c. fly

**6** — HOMOGRAPHS Question

Which word best completes both sentences below?

Our teacher gave us a _____ after the long test.

Dusty will try not to _____ his new toy.

a. break
b. hurt
c. treat

**6** — HOMOGRAPHS Answer

a. break

Cooperative Learning & Grammar
Kagan Publishing • 1 (800) 933-2667 • www.KaganOnline.com

Antonyms, Homographs, Homophones, Synonyms

**Instructions:** Cut out each card along the dotted line. Then fold each card in half so the question is on one side and the answer is on the back. Glue or tape the cards together to keep the answers and questions on opposite sides.

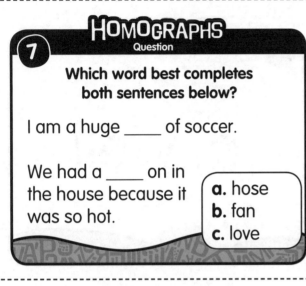

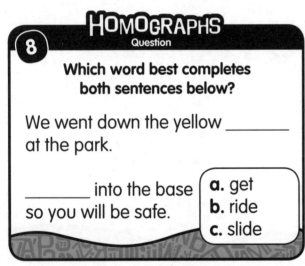

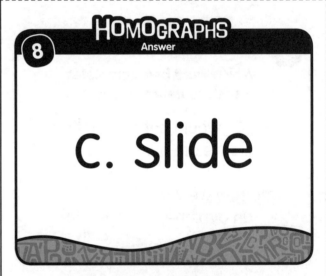

26    Antonyms, Homographs, Homophones, Synonyms

# Homographs Quiz-Quiz-Trade

**Instructions:** Cut out each card along the dotted line. Then fold each card in half so the question is on one side and the answer is on the back. Glue or tape the cards together to keep the answers and questions on opposite sides.

---

**10 — Homographs Question**

Which word best completes both sentences below?

We will have to _____ a hotel for our vacation.

I'm reading a _____ about sports.

a. get
b. box
c. book

**10 — Homographs Answer**

c. book

---

**11 — Homographs Question**

Which word best completes both sentences below?

Never _____ anyone by the way they look.

My grandpa is a _____ in a court.

a. judge
b. look
c. man

**11 — Homographs Answer**

a. judge

---

**12 — Homographs Question**

Which word best completes both sentences below?

We had to wait in a long _____ to buy a game.

Use the fishing _____ to bait the hook.

a. time
b. worm
c. line

**12 — Homographs Answer**

c. line

---

Cooperative Learning & Grammar
Antonyms, Homographs, Homophones, Synonyms

**Instructions:** Cut out each card along the dotted line. Then fold each card in half so the question is on one side and the answer is on the back. Glue or tape the cards together to keep the answers and questions on opposite sides.

### 13 — Homographs Question

Which word best completes both sentences below?

You can ____ easily when you run.

We got a flat ____ from a nail in the road.

a. tire
b. walk
c. wheel

### 13 — Homographs Answer

a. tire

### 14 — Homographs Question

Which word best completes both sentences below?

If you _____ wrong when jumping, you could hurt yourself.

My father bought 14 acres of _____.

a. run
b. grass
c. land

### 14 — Homographs Answer

c. land

### 15 — Homographs Question

Which word best completes both sentences below?

Use a _____ to light the fire.

The tennis _____ will last three hours.

a. gas
b. match
c. game

### 15 — Homographs Answer

b. match

28    Antonyms, Homographs, Homophones, Synonyms

# HOMOGRAPHS
## Quiz-Quiz-Trade

**Instructions:** Cut out each card along the dotted line. Then fold each card in half so the question is on one side and the answer is on the back. Glue or tape the cards together to keep the answers and questions on opposite sides.

### 16 — HOMOGRAPHS Question

Which word best completes both sentences below?

My sister said she felt _____ after crashing her bike.

When library books are late, you have to pay a _____.

a. fee
b. good
c. fine

### 16 — HOMOGRAPHS Answer

c. fine

### 17 — HOMOGRAPHS Question

Which word best completes both sentences below?

I love to _____ back and forth on the rope.

The baseball player will _____ the bat.

a. swing
b. hit
c. ride

### 17 — HOMOGRAPHS Answer

a. swing

### 18 — HOMOGRAPHS Question

Which word best completes both sentences below?

I will give you a rubber _____.

Jim's _____ will play at the talent show.

a. walk
b. paper
c. band

### 18 — HOMOGRAPHS Answer

c. band

**Cooperative Learning & Grammar**
Kagan Publishing • 1 (800) 933-2667 • www.KaganOnline.com

Antonyms, Homographs, Homophones, Synonyms

**Instructions:** Cut out each card along the dotted line. Then fold each card in half so the question is on one side and the answer is on the back. Glue or tape the cards together to keep the answers and questions on opposite sides.

**HOMOGRAPHS — 19 — Question**

Which word best completes both sentences below?

Do you _____ if I borrow your toys?

Everyone's _____ does not think the same way.

a. brain
b. care
c. mind

**HOMOGRAPHS — 19 — Answer**

c. mind

**HOMOGRAPHS — 20 — Question**

Which word best completes both sentences below?

I have a cat for a ____.

Lucy and Sam like to ____ dogs.

a. animal
b. pet
c. play

**HOMOGRAPHS — 20 — Answer**

b. pet

**HOMOGRAPHS — 21 — Question**

Which word best completes both sentences below?

The dog performed a _____.

John will _____ Tim into doing his work.

a. act
b. ask
c. trick

**HOMOGRAPHS — 21 — Answer**

c. trick

**Instructions:** Cut out each card along the dotted line. Then fold each card in half so the question is on one side and the answer is on the back. Glue or tape the cards together to keep the answers and questions on opposite sides.

### 22 — HOMOGRAPHS Question
Which word best completes both sentences below?

Open the window just a _____.

Troy will _____ the nuts.

a. crack
b. get
c. little

### 22 — HOMOGRAPHS Answer
a. crack

### 23 — HOMOGRAPHS Question
Which word best completes both sentences below?

I need you to go to the _____ for me.

I will _____ the toys in the box.

a. put
b. store
c. mall

### 23 — HOMOGRAPHS Answer
b. store

### 24 — HOMOGRAPHS Question
Which word best completes both sentences below?

The employees would like a _____.

We _____ the flag on the 4th of July.

a. put
b. treat
c. raise

### 24 — HOMOGRAPHS Answer
c. raise

**Cooperative Learning & Grammar**
Kagan Publishing • 1 (800) 933-2667 • www.KaganOnline.com

Antonyms, Homographs, Homophones, Synonyms  31

# Homophones
## Find-N-Fix

Name _____

**Instructions:** For each set of problems, find the incorrect sentence. Indicate which is incorrect using your Find-N-Fix cards. When your team agrees, fix the incorrect problem by writing the correct word above the homophone.

**1** In which sentence is the underlined word used incorrectly?

1. I <u>scent</u> the letter to my grandpa in the mail.
2. The red bouquet of flowers had a strong <u>scent</u>.
3. I wonder how many letters get <u>sent</u> to Santa Claus each year.

**2** In which sentence is the underlined word used incorrectly?

1. We had to <u>sell</u> all of our furniture before we moved.
2. The grocery store could <u>sell</u> all types of cereal.
3. It is hard to <u>cell</u> a home without a pool.

**3** In which sentence is the underlined word used incorrectly?

1. My little sister <u>ate</u> ten chicken nuggets for lunch.
2. The brown bear <u>eight</u> three fish.
3. Spiders have <u>eight</u> legs.

**4** In which sentence is the underlined word used incorrectly?

1. I <u>red</u> five books over the summer.
2. The <u>red</u> bird flew by our car window.
3. How many books have you <u>read</u> since last weekend?

**5** In which sentence is the underlined word used incorrectly?

1. <u>They're</u> house used to be painted blue.
2. My dogs like to chase <u>their</u> tails.
3. I think I saw a restroom over <u>there</u> near the water fountain.

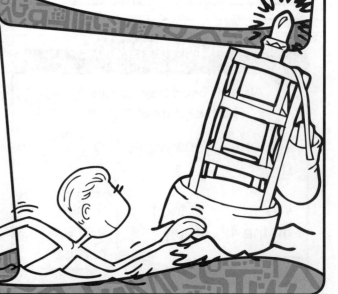

Antonyms, Homographs, Homophones, Synonyms

# Homophones
## RallyCoach/Sage-N-Scribe

**Instructions:** For each problem, circle the word to make a correct sentence. Take turns working with your partner to solve the problems using RallyCoach or Sage-N-Scribe.

## Partner A

Name _____

1. My dad has one **(son, sun)** and two daughters.
2. This weekend my mom had a yard **(sale, sail)**.
3. Najem saw a brown **(bare, bear)** in her backyard.
4. My sister was a **(which, witch)** for Halloween this year.
5. At dinner I **(ate, eight)** three hotdogs.
6. The dog kept chasing **(it's, its)** tail.
7. **(Oh, Owe)** what a beautiful day!
8. My dad bought my mom a **(flour, flower)** for their anniversary.
9. The bird **(flew, flu)** away when the cat climbed up the tree.
10. I like my hamburgers **(plain, plane)**.
11. When the storm **(blew, blue)** in, we had to leave the pool.

## Partner B

Name _____

1. **(There, They're)** are twelve girls in my class.
2. The **(sent, scent)** of the perfume was very strong.
3. My dad got a **(whole, hole)** in one during his golf game yesterday.
4. The piano recital lasted one **(our, hour)**.
5. Sally's dad had to fix a loose **(bored, board)** in her clubhouse.
6. It was so bright outside I could hardly **(see, sea)**.
7. My mom made me **(cell, sell)** all my action figures in the garage sale.
8. The cat's **(tale, tail)** got stuck in the door.
9. The teacher gave the students **(to, two)** worksheets for homework.
10. The little **(ant, aunt)** picked up the big crumb.
11. There was a **(deer, dear)** in the middle of the road.

# Homographs
## RallyCoach/Sage-N-Scribe

**Instructions:** For each problem, identify the sentence with the underlined word that has the same meaning as the underlined word in the first sentence. Take turns with your partner to solve each problem using RallyCoach or Sage-N-Scribe.

## Partner A

Name _____

**1.** I need to set my watch to beep when it is time to go to school.
- a. Please watch your little sister while I do the laundry.
- b. My uncle gave me a pocket watch for completing my boy scout project.
- c. I need to watch for my friend's signal telling me the coast is clear.

**2.** What page is the homework?
- a. Can you page the doctor for me?
- b. The page delivered the message to the lawyer's office.
- c. My teacher asked me to read to page fifty-six of my reading book.

**3.** Kelly is coming over to play baseball with me.
- a. The school play is about sharing.
- b. I can't wait to play football in the fall.
- c. The coach described a play to win the game.

**4.** The mosquito bit my arm leaving a mark.
- a. May I have a bit of honey in my tea?
- b. The drill bit broke in the wood.
- c. The horse bit at the apple because he was hungry.

## Partner B

Name _____

**1.** The rabbits were kept in a pen for the kids to observe.
- a. The goat pen had a hole in it.
- b. My ink pen is not working.
- c. The author will pen his name on all of his books.

**2.** The principal will present the spelling bee winner with a trophy.
- a. Did this story take place in the present, past, or future?
- b. I got my mom a present for mother's day.
- c. My teacher will present a certificate for the cleanest desk.

**3.** Don't forget to close the refrigerator door when you are finished.
- a. The boy sat close to the whiteboard.
- b. Larry, please close your math book.
- c. We are getting close to arriving at our destination.

**4.** The class president will address the student body during the assembly.
- a. Can you please address this envelope?
- b. The president will address the public in his speech.
- c. What is your address to send you the invitation?

34  Antonyms, Homographs, Homophones, Synonyms

**Cooperative Learning & Grammar**
Kagan Publishing • 1 (800) 933-2667 • www.KaganOnline.com

Name _____

**Instructions:** Pair up and take turns writing a synonym, antonym, or homonym for the word in the box. Don't forget to get your partner's initials.

| # | Prompt |
|---|---|
| 1 | Synonym for pretty: |
| 2 | Antonym for happy: |
| 3 | Homonym for bare: |
| 4 | Synonym for sleepy: |
| 5 | Antonym for up: |
| 6 | Synonym for dirty: |
| 7 | Antonym for closed: |
| 8 | Homonym for pair: |
| 9 | Antonym for sunny: |
| 10 | Antonym for night: |
| 11 | Synonym for tardy: |
| 12 | Antonym for above: |
| 13 | Homonym for sail: |
| 14 | Antonym for closed: |
| 15 | Antonym for ugly: |
| 16 | Synonym for ill: |
| 17 | Antonym for wet: |
| 18 | Homonym for where: |
| 19 | Synonym for mad: |
| 20 | Antonym for fast: |
| 21 | Synonym for little: |
| 22 | Antonym for quiet: |
| 23 | Homonym for there: |
| 24 | Synonym for huge: |
| 25 | Antonym for exciting: |

*Cooperative Learning & Grammar*
Kagan Publishing • 1 (800) 933-2667 • www.KaganOnline.com

Antonyms, Homographs, Homophones, Synonyms

# Grammar Skills 2
# PARTS OF SPEECH

- **Verb Tense** (Find Someone Who) .................. 38
- **Verb Tense** (Find-N-Fix) ............................. 39
- **Verb Usage** (Showdown/Fan-N-Pick) .... 40–42
- **Helping Verbs** (Find Someone Who) ........... 43
- **Helping Verbs**
  (Showdown/Fan-N-Pick) ..................... 44–46
- **Irregular Verbs**
  (RallyCoach/Sage-N-Scribe) ..................... 47
- **Irregular Verbs** (Find Someone Who) ........... 48
- **Action Verbs** (RallyCoach/Sage-N-Scribe) .... 49
- **Action or Being Verbs** (Find Someone Who) 50
- **Comparative & Superlative Adjectives**
  (RallyCoach/Sage-N-Scribe) ..................... 51
- **Descriptive Adjectives**
  (Find Someone Who) .............................. 52
- **Adjectives** (Showdown/Fan-N-Pick) ....... 53–55
- **Adverbs** (Rally Coach/Sage-N-Scribe) .......... 56
- **Adverbs** (Find Someone Who) ..................... 57
- **Adverbs** (Showdown/Fan-N-Pick) .......... 58–60
- **Nouns** (RallyCoach/Sage-N-Scribe) .............. 61
- **Nouns** (Find Someone Who) .................. 62–63
- **Common & Proper Nouns**
  (Mix-N-Match) .................................... 64–67
- **Parts of Speech**
  (RallyCoach/Sage-N-Scribe) ................. 68–69
- **Parts of Speech**
  (Find Someone Who) .............................. 70
- **Parts of Speech**
  (Quiz-Quiz-Trade) .............................. 71–77
- **Plural Nouns: Adding -es and -s**
  (RallyCoach/Sage-N-Scribe) ..................... 78
- **Plural Nouns: Adding -es and -s**
  (Find Someone Who) .............................. 79
- **Plural Nouns: Words ending in -y**
  (RallyCoach/Sage-N-Scribe) ..................... 80
- **Plural Nouns: Words ending in -y**
  (Find Someone Who) .............................. 81
- **Plural Nouns: Words ending in -f or -fe**
  (RallyCoach/Sage-N-Scribe) ..................... 82

- **Plural Nouns: Words ending in -f or -fe**
  (Find Someone Who) .............................. 83
- **Irregular Plural Nouns**
  (RallyCoach/Sage-N-Scribe) ..................... 84
- **Irregular Plural Nouns**
  (Find Someone Who) .............................. 85
- **Plural Nouns: Review** (Find-N-Fix) ............. 86
- **Plural Nouns: Review**
  (Find Someone Who) .............................. 87
- **Plural Nouns** (Mix-N-Match) ................ 88–91
- **Possessive Nouns** (Find-N-Fix) .................. 92
- **Possessive Nouns**
  (RallyCoach/Sage-N-Scribe) ..................... 93
- **Possessive Nouns** (Find Someone Who) ...... 94
- **Possessive Nouns** (Quiz-Quiz-Trade) .... 95–102
- **Possessive Pronouns**
  (Find Someone Who) ............................ 103
- **Pronouns** (RallyCoach/Sage-N-Scribe) ....... 104
- **Pronouns** (Showdown/Fan-N-Pick) ..... 105–107
- **Pronouns** (Quiz-Quiz-Trade) ............... 108–114
- **Suffixes** (RallyCoach/Sage-N-Scribe) .......... 115
- **Suffixes & Prefixes**
  (Find Someone Who) ........................ 116–117
- **Prefix, Suffix & Root Words**
  (Quiz-Quiz-Trade) ............................ 118–125
- **Articles** (Find-N-Fix) .............................. 126
- **Articles** (RallyCoach/Sage-N-Scribe) ........... 127
- **Compound Words**
  (RallyCoach/Sage-N-Scribe) ..................... 128
- **Compound Words** (Find Someone Who) ..... 129
- **Compound Words** (Mix-N-Match) ...... 130–133
- **Contractions** (Find-N-Fix) ....................... 134
- **Contractions**
  (RallyCoach/Sage-N-Scribe) ............... 135–138
- **Contractions** (Find Someone Who) ..... 139–140
- **Contractions** (Quiz-Quiz-Trade) .......... 141–156
- **Prepositions** (RallyCoach/Sage-N-Scribe) .... 157

- **Answer Key** ................................... 239–246

# Verb Tense
## Find Someone Who

**Name** _____

**Instructions:** Pair up and take turns solving one problem on each other's sheet by underlining the verb in the sentence, then writing the verb's tense (present tense, past tense, or future tense) in the box provided. Don't forget to get your partner's initials.

| # | Sentence | Verb Tense | Initials |
|---|---|---|---|
| 1 | Scientists view tiny things with microscopes. | | |
| 2 | Many microscopes will have only one lens each. | | |
| 3 | Some people call glaciers great sheets of ice. | | |
| 4 | Inventors will complete their work using microscopes. | | |
| 5 | Many of us have studied Martin Luther King Jr. | | |
| 6 | He never received one tardy at school. | | |
| 7 | John will complete the marathon on Sunday. | | |
| 8 | Ocean waves will cut caves in some icebergs. | | |
| 9 | Roses lined the fence outside the neighbor's home. | | |
| 10 | Sue will write a letter to the president. | | |

# Verb Tense Find-N-Fix

Name _____

**Instructions:** For each set of problems, find the incorrect sentence. Indicate which is incorrect using your Find-N-Fix cards. When your team agrees, fix the incorrect problem by writing the correct verb tense above the incorrect word.

**1** In which sentence is the verb tense not correct?

1. Mr. Brown run a 5K marathon.
2. Yesterday we swam at the pool.
3. I read a good book last week.

**2** In which sentence is the verb tense not correct?

1. I walked to school yesterday.
2. We grown plants in our garden.
3. Billy jumped on the couch.

**3** In which sentence is the verb tense not correct?

1. Do you care about animals?
2. We writted a book about mammals.
3. Jane will swim this weekend.

**4** In which sentence is the verb tense not correct?

1. It land over the fence.
2. He will slide into home plate.
3. The crowd screams wildly.

**5** In which sentence is the verb tense not correct?

1. The door will shut on its own.
2. Sam plays quarterback on the team.
3. My dog will jumps 25 inches into the air.

Cooperative Learning & Grammar
Kagan Publishing • 1 (800) 933-2667 • www.KaganOnline.com

**Instructions:** Copy one set of cards for each team. Cut out each card along the dotted line. Give each team a set of cards to play Fan-N-Pick or Showdown.

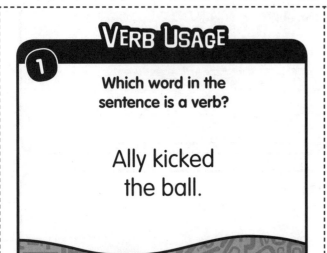

**VERB USAGE**

**1**

Which word in the sentence is a verb?

Ally kicked the ball.

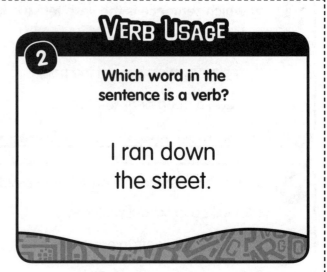

**VERB USAGE**

**2**

Which word in the sentence is a verb?

I ran down the street.

**VERB USAGE**

**3**

Which word in the sentence is a verb?

My dad chopped down the tree.

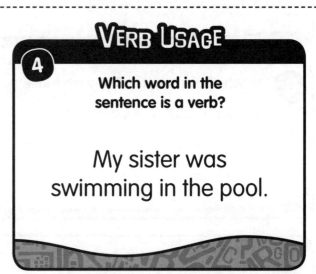

**VERB USAGE**

**4**

Which word in the sentence is a verb?

My sister was swimming in the pool.

**VERB USAGE**

**5**

Which word in the sentence is a verb?

Joel threw the ball to Mary.

**VERB USAGE**

**6**

Which word in the sentence is a verb?

The dog bit the young girl.

# Verb Usage
## Showdown/Fan-N-Pick

**Instructions:** Copy one set of cards for each team. Cut out each card along the dotted line. Give each team a set of cards to play Fan-N-Pick or Showdown.

---

### Verb Usage
**7.** Which verb would best complete the sentence?

Santa Claus was _____ down the chimney.

- a. jumped
- b. jump
- c. jumping

---

### Verb Usage
**8.** Which verb would best complete the sentence?

Yesterday Joe _____ in the pool.

- a. swim
- b. swimming
- c. swam

---

### Verb Usage
**9.** Which verb would best complete the sentence?

Joe and Sally will _____ to the movies tomorrow.

- a. walking
- b. walked
- c. walk

---

### Verb Usage
**10.** Which verb would best complete the sentence?

I _____ a piece of candy this morning.

- a. eat
- b. ate
- c. eaten

---

### Verb Usage
**11.** Which verb would best complete the sentence?

My mom was _____ a cake.

- a. bake
- b. baked
- c. baking

---

### Verb Usage
**12.** Which verb would best complete the sentence?

The dog _____ the ball in his mouth.

- a. caught
- b. catch
- c. catching

---

Cooperative Learning & Grammar
Kagan Publishing • 1 (800) 933-2667 • www.KaganOnline.com

Parts of Speech  **41**

**Instructions:** Copy one set of cards for each team. Cut out each card along the dotted line. Give each team a set of cards to play Fan-N-Pick or Showdown.

---

### Verb Usage

**13.** Is the underlined word a noun or a verb?

My dad paddled the <u>boat</u> to shore.

---

### Verb Usage

**14.** Is the underlined word a noun or a verb?

We built a <u>sand</u> <u>castle</u> at the beach.

---

### Verb Usage

**15.** Is the underlined word a noun or a verb?

My cat <u>scratched</u> the couch.

---

### Verb Usage

**16.** Is the underlined word a noun or a verb?

The dog <u>ran</u> down the street.

---

### Verb Usage

**17.** Is the underlined word a noun or a verb?

We had to <u>run</u> five laps in P.E.

---

### Verb Usage

**18.** Is the underlined word a noun or a verb?

The boy <u>licked</u> his sucker.

# HELPING VERBS
## Find Someone Who

Name _____

**Instructions:** Pair up and take turns underlining the helping verb(s) in the sentence. Don't forget to get your partner's initials.

| 1. Maria might spend the night. | 2. I can do my homework later. | 3. What shall we buy at the mall today? |
|---|---|---|
| Initials: | Initials: | Initials: |
| 4. Jamar has been working much too hard. | 5. Cindee has missed three days of school. | 6. When will you finish the newspaper? |
| Initials: | Initials: | Initials: |
| 7. Michelle has been writing a report on turtles. | 8. Malee should have eaten her dinner. | 9. My mom has been cooking all day long. |
| Initials: | Initials: | Initials: |

# Helping Verbs
## Showdown/Fan-N-Pick

**Instructions:** Copy one set of cards for each team. Cut out each card along the dotted line. Give each team a set of cards to play Fan-N-Pick or Showdown.

---

**HELPING VERBS**

**1.** Which word in the sentence is a helping verb?

Beth and Cindy had gone to the library.

---

**HELPING VERBS**

**2.** Which word in the sentence is a helping verb?

Denzel will eat spaghetti and meatballs for dinner tonight.

---

**HELPING VERBS**

**3.** Which word in the sentence is a helping verb?

Those quick raccoons have run into the sewer.

---

**HELPING VERBS**

**4.** Which word in the sentence is a helping verb?

Maggie is walking to the park.

---

**HELPING VERBS**

**5.** Which word in the sentence is a helping verb?

I am going away for the weekend.

---

**HELPING VERBS**

**6.** Which word in the sentence is a helping verb?

The dogs are sleeping in their beds.

# Helping Verbs
## Showdown/Fan-N-Pick

**Instructions:** Copy one set of cards for each team. Cut out each card along the dotted line. Give each team a set of cards to play Fan-N-Pick or Showdown.

---

**HELPING VERBS — 7**

Which word in the sentence is a helping verb?

Gracie was studying for an hour.

---

**HELPING VERBS — 8**

Which word in the sentence is a helping verb?

Norman has built a huge sand castle on the beach.

---

**HELPING VERBS — 9**

Which word in the sentence is a helping verb?

My sister will be ten years old tomorrow.

---

**HELPING VERBS — 10**

Which word in the sentence is a helping verb?

Chris can swim in the pool after lunch.

---

**HELPING VERBS — 11**

Which word in the sentence is a helping verb?

Omar was mowing the lawn when I arrived.

---

**HELPING VERBS — 12**

Which word in the sentence is a helping verb?

The truck is making an awful noise.

**Instructions:** Copy one set of cards for each team. Cut out each card along the dotted line. Give each team a set of cards to play Fan-N-Pick or Showdown.

---

**HELPING VERBS**

**13.** Which word in the sentence is a helping verb?

Jacob should fix his bicycle.

---

**HELPING VERBS**

**14.** Which word in the sentence is a helping verb?

My friend Sara had already left when I called.

---

**HELPING VERBS**

**15.** Which word in the sentence is a helping verb?

Trudy must bake the cake tomorrow.

---

**HELPING VERBS**

**16.** Which word in the sentence is a helping verb?

Jessica has always gotten good grades.

---

**HELPING VERBS**

**17.** Which word in the sentence is a helping verb?

Has the baby been cranky all day?

---

**HELPING VERBS**

**18.** Which word in the sentence is a helping verb?

Jade and Mark are arguing about the game.

# Irregular Verbs
## RallyCoach/Sage-N-Scribe

**Instructions:** Write each verb in the past tense form in the box provided. Take turns working with your partner to solve the problems using RallyCoach or Sage-N-Scribe.

### Partner A

Name _____

| # | Verb | Past Tense |
|---|------|------------|
| 1 | grow | |
| 2 | run | |
| 3 | eat | |
| 4 | give | |
| 5 | break | |
| 6 | swim | |
| 7 | write | |
| 8 | see | |
| 9 | go | |
| 10 | come | |

### Partner B

Name _____

| # | Verb | Past Tense |
|---|------|------------|
| 1 | drive | |
| 2 | throw | |
| 3 | dive | |
| 4 | tell | |
| 5 | fall | |
| 6 | get | |
| 7 | catch | |
| 8 | find | |
| 9 | sleep | |
| 10 | win | |

# Irregular Verbs
## Find Someone Who

Name _____

**Instructions:** Pair up and take turns circling the correct form of the verb in the sentence. Don't forget to use the information in the parentheses and to get your partner's initials.

**1** The photographer **(took, taken)** my picture.

Initials

**2** They **(went, gone)** to Lake Erie.

Initials

**3** Gary was **(gave, given)** third place in the eating contest.

Initials

**4** Darcee **(ate, eaten)** a peanut butter sandwich for lunch.

Initials

**5** We **(saw, seen)** the greatest tennis match.

Initials

**6** The third graders **(took, taken)** a field trip today.

Initials

**7** My family has **(go, gone)** to the Museum of Science.

Initials

**8** Julie **(came, come)** to my baseball game.

Initials

**9** I **(broke, broken)** my leg while skiing in Colorado.

Initials

48  Parts of Speech

*Cooperative Learning & Grammar*
Kagan Publishing • 1 (800) 933-2667 • www.KaganOnline.com

# Action Verbs
## RallyCoach/Sage-N-Scribe

**Instructions:** Take turns working with your partner using RallyCoach or Sage-N-Scribe. On your turn, find the next action word in the box and write it on the lines below.

1. raced
2. washed
3. moon
4. viewed
5. car
6. go
7. enjoyed
8. tennis
9. about
10. eraser
11. paints
12. people
13. worked
14. white
15. ruler
16. adored
17. sang
18. tiny
19. swam
20. delicious
21. pretty
22. roared
23. ate
24. looked
25. park
26. divided
27. jumped
28. slipped

**PARTNER A**

Name _____

**PARTNER B**

Name _____

# Action or Being Verbs
## Find Someone Who

Name _____

**Instructions:** Pair up and take turns underlining the verb in each sentence. Then write if the verb is an action or being verb in the box provided. Don't forget to get your partner's initials.

| | Sentence | Action or Being Verb | Initials |
|---|---|---|---|
| 1 | Many people play summer sports. | | |
| 2 | Skating is an important part of ice hockey. | | |
| 3 | He raced to the water. | | |
| 4 | The landing is difficult. | | |
| 5 | The Confederate Army was on the march. | | |
| 6 | Spectators watch as the skier takes the platform. | | |
| 7 | The contestants are in the Summer Olympics. | | |
| 8 | Both men and women were there. | | |
| 9 | People watch the Olympics on TV. | | |
| 10 | Jet skis are fun, too. | | |

# Comparative & Superlative Adjectives
## RallyCoach/Sage-N-Scribe

**Instructions:** In the sentences below, circle the correct form of the adjective in the parentheses. Take turns working with your partner to solve the problems using RallyCoach or Sage-N-Scribe.

## Partner A

Name _____

1. Tim is the **(tallest, taller)** boy in our class.
2. The lemonade is **(tastiest, tastier)** than soda.
3. I think math is the **(harder, hardest)** subject in school.
4. The truck was the **(bigger, biggest)** car in the school parking lot.
5. Martin is **(oldest, older)** than Maria.
6. This is the **(warmest, warmer)** blanket in the house.
7. That was the **(big, bigger, biggest)** hot fudge sundae I have ever eaten.
8. Marsha is **(happy, happiest, happier)** than Jan right now.
9. This is a very **(long, longer, longest)** fishing pole.
10. Mr. Jones is the **(nice, nicest, nicer)** teacher in the school.

## Partner B

Name _____

1. Katrina ran even **(fast, faster, faster)** than I did.
2. January is the **(coldest, colder)** month of the year.
3. A steak knife is **(sharper, sharpest)** than a butter knife.
4. Isn't he the **(nicest, nicer)** boy you have ever met?
5. Do you think a snake is **(slow, slower, slowest)** than an owl?
6. Jim has the **(big, biggest, bigger)** feet in the family.
7. Lucy's shirt was the **(long, longest, longer)** shirt in the class.
8. Mrs. Smith's desk is **(larger, largest, large)** than her students' desks.
9. Shirley has the **(fancier, fanciest)** dress at the ball.
10. Milo's cat is **(fatter, fattest, fat)** than Sarah's dog.

# Descriptive Adjectives
## Find Someone Who

Name _____

**Instructions:** Pair up and take turns circling the descriptive adjectives and underlining the nouns they modify in the sentences below. Don't forget to get your partner's initials.

**Initials**

1. A tornado is a terrifying occurrence.

2. A large earthquake at sea can generate giant waves.

3. Precious coral has a red color.

4. Animals with shells have lived in the deep sea for millions of years.

5. Corals look like small flowers.

6. The small boat foundered on the dark sea.

7. The back room was filled with large, yellow rain boots.

8. My husband mows an intricate pattern into the grass.

9. Sam listened to the muffled sounds of his broken radio.

10. The circle-shaped balloon floated over the tall treetops.

# ADJECTIVES
## Showdown/Fan-N-Pick

**Instructions:** Copy one set of cards for each team. Cut out each card along the dotted line. Give each team a set of cards to play Fan-N-Pick or Showdown.

---

**ADJECTIVES 1**

Which word in the sentence is an adjective?

We spilled milk on the black floor.

---

**ADJECTIVES 2**

Which word in the sentence is an adjective?

Sally has five brothers.

---

**ADJECTIVES 3**

Which word in the sentence is an adjective?

The lake was full of cold water.

---

**ADJECTIVES 4**

Which word in the sentence is an adjective?

The girl was wearing a yellow dress.

---

**ADJECTIVES 5**

Which word in the sentence is an adjective?

We saw the saddest clown at the circus.

---

**ADJECTIVES 6**

Which word in the sentence is an adjective?

Ms. Kern has on the reddest dress I have ever seen.

---

*Cooperative Learning & Grammar*
Kagan Publishing • 1 (800) 933-2667 • www.KaganOnline.com

Parts of Speech 53

# ADJECTIVES
## Showdown/Fan-N-Pick

**Instructions:** Copy one set of cards for each team. Cut out each card along the dotted line. Give each team a set of cards to play Fan-N-Pick or Showdown.

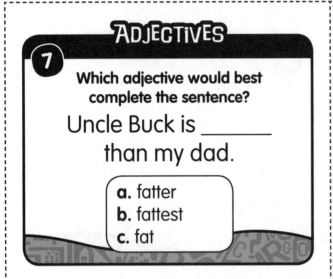

**7.** Which adjective would best complete the sentence?

Uncle Buck is _____ than my dad.

a. fatter
b. fattest
c. fat

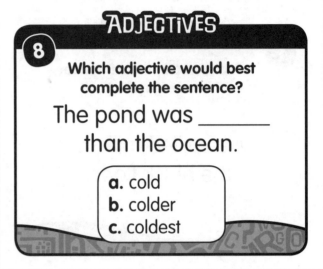

**8.** Which adjective would best complete the sentence?

The pond was _____ than the ocean.

a. cold
b. colder
c. coldest

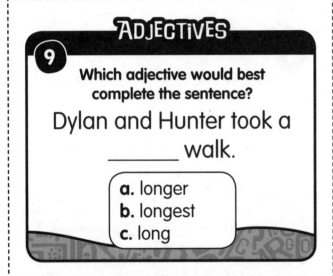

**9.** Which adjective would best complete the sentence?

Dylan and Hunter took a _____ walk.

a. longer
b. longest
c. long

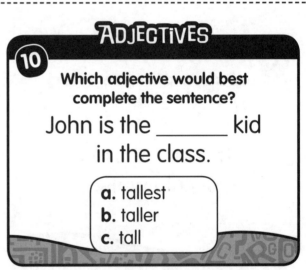

**10.** Which adjective would best complete the sentence?

John is the _____ kid in the class.

a. tallest
b. taller
c. tall

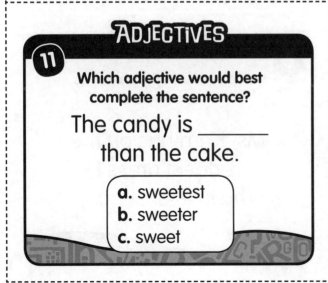

**11.** Which adjective would best complete the sentence?

The candy is _____ than the cake.

a. sweetest
b. sweeter
c. sweet

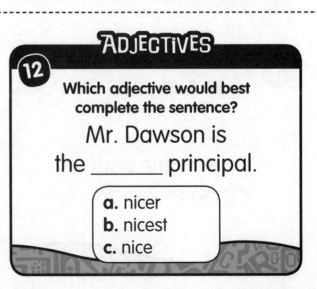

**12.** Which adjective would best complete the sentence?

Mr. Dawson is the _____ principal.

a. nicer
b. nicest
c. nice

# Adjectives
## Showdown/Fan-N-Pick

**Instructions:** Copy one set of cards for each team. Cut out each card along the dotted line. Give each team a set of cards to play Fan-N-Pick or Showdown.

---

**ADJECTIVES — 13**

Is the underlined word a noun or an adjective?

Yesterday my family went to <u>Taco Shack</u> for dinner.

---

**ADJECTIVES — 14**

Is the underlined word a noun or an adjective?

The bad thunderstorm caused the <u>tree</u> to fall over.

---

**ADJECTIVES — 15**

Is the underlined word a noun or an adjective?

The remote control was under the <u>brown</u> couch.

---

**ADJECTIVES — 16**

Is the underlined word a noun or an adjective?

The <u>lazy</u> bear slept all winter.

---

**ADJECTIVES — 17**

Is the underlined word a noun or an adjective?

<u>Coach Hart</u> made us run ten laps in P.E.

---

**ADJECTIVES — 18**

Is the underlined word a noun or an adjective?

The <u>generous</u> boy gave his sister a sucker.

---

*Cooperative Learning & Grammar*
Kagan Publishing • 1 (800) 933-2667 • www.KaganOnline.com

# ADVERBS
## RallyCoach/Sage-N-Scribe

**Instructions:** In the sentences below, write an adverb on the line to complete the sentence. The word underneath the line indicates the kind of adverb to write. You can only use an adverb once. Take turns working with your partner to solve the problems using RallyCoach or Sage-N-Scribe.

### Partner A
Name _____

1. Our team played _____ (where).
2. Brian writes _____ (how).
3. The cows move _____ (how).
4. We'll be leaving _____ (when).
5. We have two bedrooms _____ (where).
6. Jim ran _____ (how) down the street.
7. The man went _____ (where) with his paper.
8. The cat purred _____ (how).
9. Sammy spoke _____ (how).
10. The sign goes _____ (where).

### Partner B
Name _____

1. John got his bicycle _____ (when).
2. We _____ (how) finished the game.
3. Jack went home _____ (when).
4. I washed my dog _____ (when).
5. _____ (how), I cleaned my room.
6. Doug took his wagon _____ (where).
7. The choir sang _____ (how).
8. We ran _____ (how).
9. The mouse crept out _____ (how).
10. _____ (when), I baked cookies.

56 Parts of Speech • Cooperative Learning & Grammar • Kagan Publishing • 1 (800) 933-2667 • www.KaganOnline.com

# ADVERBS
## Find Someone Who

**Name** _____

**Instructions:** Pair up and take turns circling the adverb in each sentence. Don't forget to get your partner's initials.

1. I carefully put the vase on the counter.

2. My mom went upstairs to get my sister who was crying.

3. The boy ran quickly down the street.

4. We went on a hike yesterday at camp.

5. The crab ran under the rock.

6. My mom will bring in my birthday cupcakes tomorrow.

7. The boys noisily hammered the piece of wood.

8. Susan generously shared her cookies with the little girl.

9. My mom told me to practice my instrument quietly in the garage.

# ADVERBS
## Showdown/Fan-N-Pick

**Instructions:** Copy one set of cards for each team. Cut out each card along the dotted line. Give each team a set of cards to play Fan-N-Pick or Showdown.

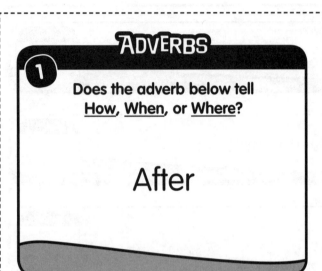

**1. ADVERBS** — Does the adverb below tell How, When, or Where?

After

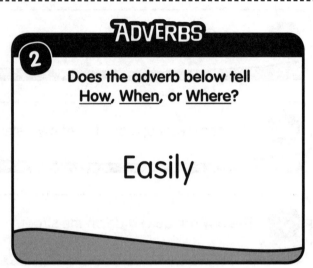

**2. ADVERBS** — Does the adverb below tell How, When, or Where?

Easily

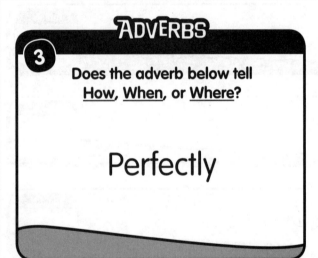

**3. ADVERBS** — Does the adverb below tell How, When, or Where?

Perfectly

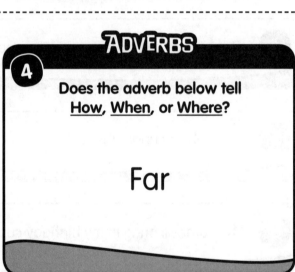

**4. ADVERBS** — Does the adverb below tell How, When, or Where?

Far

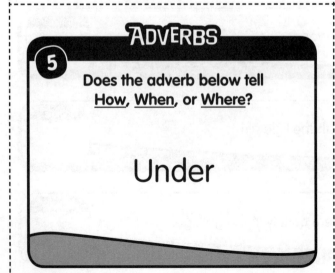

**5. ADVERBS** — Does the adverb below tell How, When, or Where?

Under

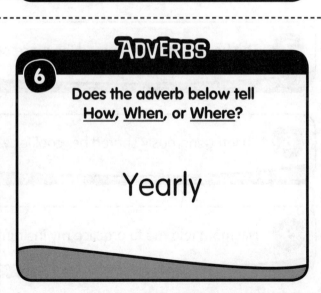

**6. ADVERBS** — Does the adverb below tell How, When, or Where?

Yearly

# ADVERBS
## Showdown/Fan-N-Pick

**Instructions:** Copy one set of cards for each team. Cut out each card along the dotted line. Give each team a set of cards to play Fan-N-Pick or Showdown.

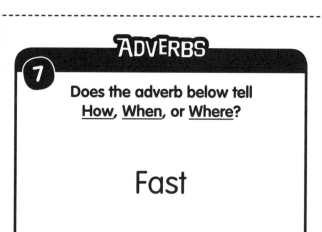

**7** — ADVERBS: Does the adverb below tell How, When, or Where? **Fast**

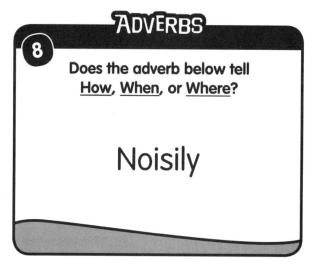

**8** — ADVERBS: Does the adverb below tell How, When, or Where? **Noisily**

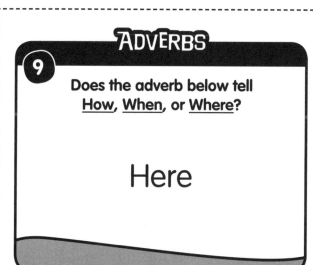

**9** — ADVERBS: Does the adverb below tell How, When, or Where? **Here**

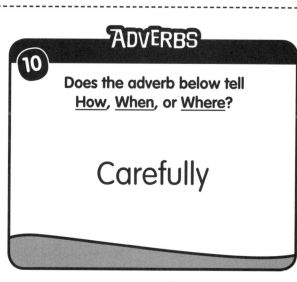

**10** — ADVERBS: Does the adverb below tell How, When, or Where? **Carefully**

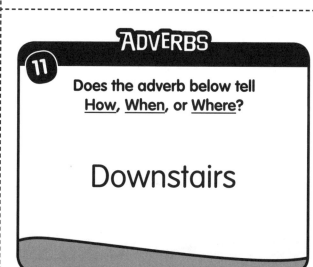

**11** — ADVERBS: Does the adverb below tell How, When, or Where? **Downstairs**

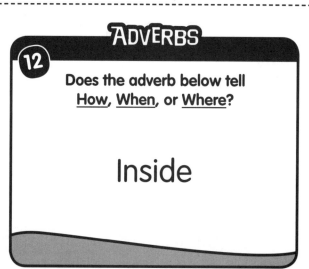

**12** — ADVERBS: Does the adverb below tell How, When, or Where? **Inside**

*Cooperative Learning & Grammar*
Kagan Publishing • 1 (800) 933-2667 • www.KaganOnline.com

# ADVERBS
## Showdown/Fan-N-Pick

**Instructions:** Copy one set of cards for each team. Cut out each card along the dotted line. Give each team a set of cards to play Fan-N-Pick or Showdown.

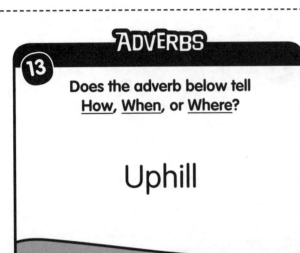

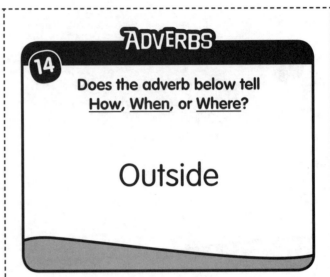

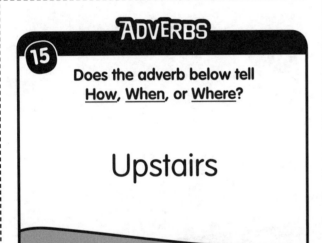

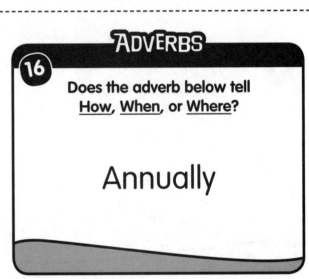

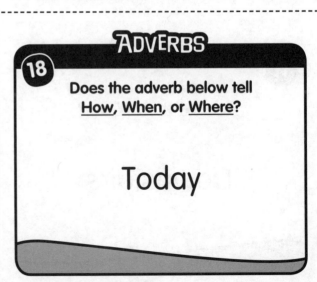

# NOUNS
## RallyCoach/Sage-N-Scribe

**Instructions:** In the sentences below, circle all the nouns in each sentence. Take turns answering the questions with your partner using RallyCoach or Sage-N-Scribe.

## PARTNER A

Name _____

1. The dog found a red rope to play with.
2. Michelle will get a hamburger at Burger Barn after school.
3. The brown cow ate grass for hours.
4. Susan will be leaving for vacation next week.
5. How many brothers do you have?
6. The mom bought the new baby a green blanket.
7. The deer search for food in the meadow.
8. When Tommy grows up, he wants to be an astronaut.
9. Mrs. Barnhart taught the class how to make tornados in a bottle.
10. The stop sign toppled over in the big storm.

## PARTNER B

Name _____

1. The green bicycle crashed into the tree.
2. Cameron cried for his mother as she left the day care.
3. The blue pillow was his favorite to sleep on.
4. The cars zoomed past the horrible accident.
5. What type of music will be heard during the concert?
6. Jenna and Ana will be dancing in the recital this Saturday.
7. Reed wore the gray shirt on his first day of school.
8. The police officer had to arrest the speeding man.
9. Skunks live in many tight places.
10. Steven cooked spaghetti for his parents.

**Cooperative Learning & Grammar**
Kagan Publishing • 1 (800) 933-2667 • www.KaganOnline.com

Parts of Speech

# Nouns
## Find Someone Who

**Name** _____

**Instructions:** Pair up and take turns identifying the underlined noun as a person, place, or thing. Write your answer on the line provided. Don't forget to get your partner's initials.

**1.** The <u>oven</u> will cook the cake at 350 degrees F.

_____ Initials

**2.** The gray striped cat got stuck under the <u>car</u>.

_____ Initials

**3.** Gatlin and <u>Mary</u> walked to the park even with the hot temperature.

_____ Initials

**4.** The <u>classroom</u> was full of empty desks.

_____ Initials

**5.** The train <u>conductor</u> lost his hat in the strong wind.

_____ Initials

**6.** John found an empty black <u>briefcase</u> on the curb.

_____ Initials

**7.** The newborn baby had hiccups after drinking his <u>bottle</u>.

_____ Initials

**8.** <u>Mrs. Carter</u> took the class out for an extra recess.

_____ Initials

**9.** Each summer our family attends church camp in <u>Iowa</u>.

_____ Initials

Parts of Speech

**Cooperative Learning & Grammar**
Kagan Publishing • 1 (800) 933-2667 • www.KaganOnline.com

# NOUNS
## Find Someone Who

**Name** _____

**Instructions:** Pair up and take turns writing a noun in the blank that best completes the sentence. Don't forget to get your partner's initials.

**Initials**

1. _____ (Noun) are big and powerful, but they can also be gentle.

2. Brian had to clean his _____ (Noun) and do his homework.

3. Emily ran down to the _____ (Noun) and saw seashells everywhere.

4. We already have learned some interesting facts about _____ (Noun).

5. _____ (Noun) is located on the continent of Europe.

6. What _____ (Noun) is farthest from the sun?

7. _____ (Noun) is the coldest time of the year.

8. An (a) _____ (Noun) is a frightening occurrence.

9. I love watching a _____ (Noun).

10. Some _____ (Noun) discovered important medical facts with a microscope.

**Cooperative Learning & Grammar**
Kagan Publishing • 1 (800) 933-2667 • www.KaganOnline.com

Parts of Speech  63

# Common & Proper Nouns
## Mix-N-Match

**Instructions:** Cut out the cards on the dotted line. Give one card to each student. Distribute cards in sequence so for every student with a Proper Noun card, there is a student with a matching Common Noun card.

---

**COMMON & PROPER NOUNS**

What is the common noun for the following word?

**Century Elementary**

*Proper Noun*

---

**COMMON & PROPER NOUNS**

What is a proper noun for the following word?

**school**

*Common Noun*

---

**COMMON & PROPER NOUNS**

What is the common noun for the following word?

**Officer Buckle**

*Proper Noun*

---

**COMMON & PROPER NOUNS**

What is a proper noun for the following word?

**police officer**

*Common Noun*

---

**COMMON & PROPER NOUNS**

What is the common noun for the following word?

**The United States of America**

*Proper Noun*

---

**COMMON & PROPER NOUNS**

What is a proper noun for the following word?

**country**

*Common Noun*

---

**64** Parts of Speech

*Cooperative Learning & Grammar*
Kagan Publishing • 1 (800) 933-2667 • www.KaganOnline.com

# Common & Proper Nouns
## Mix-N-Match

**Instructions:** Cut out the cards on the dotted line. Give one card to each student. Distribute cards in sequence so for every student with a Proper Noun card, there is a student with a matching Common Noun card.

---

**COMMON & PROPER NOUNS**

What is the common noun for the following word?

**Chicago**

*Proper Noun*

---

**COMMON & PROPER NOUNS**

What is a proper noun for the following word?

**city**

*Common Noun*

---

**COMMON & PROPER NOUNS**

What is the common noun for the following word?

**Horrible Harry and the Dead Letters**

*Proper Noun*

---

**COMMON & PROPER NOUNS**

What is a proper noun for the following word?

**book**

*Common Noun*

---

**COMMON & PROPER NOUNS**

What is the common noun for the following word?

**California**

*Proper Noun*

---

**COMMON & PROPER NOUNS**

What is a proper noun for the following word?

**state**

*Common Noun*

---

*Cooperative Learning & Grammar*
Kagan Publishing • 1 (800) 933-2667 • www.KaganOnline.com

# Common & Proper Nouns
## Mix-N-Match

**Instructions:** Cut out the cards on the dotted line. Give one card to each student. Distribute cards in sequence so for every student with a Proper Noun card, there is a student with a matching Common Noun card.

---

**COMMON & PROPER NOUNS**

What is the common noun for the following word?

**Burger Barn**

*Proper Noun*

---

**COMMON & PROPER NOUNS**

What is a proper noun for the following word?

**restaurant**

*Common Noun*

---

**COMMON & PROPER NOUNS**

What is the common noun for the following word?

**Mars**

*Proper Noun*

---

**COMMON & PROPER NOUNS**

What is a proper noun for the following word?

**planet**

*Common Noun*

---

**COMMON & PROPER NOUNS**

What is the common noun for the following word?

**Monday**

*Proper Noun*

---

**COMMON & PROPER NOUNS**

What is a proper noun for the following word?

**day of the week**

*Common Noun*

# Common & Proper Nouns
## Mix-N-Match

**Instructions:** Cut out the cards on the dotted line. Give one card to each student. Distribute cards in sequence so for every student with a Proper Noun card, there is a student with a matching Common Noun card.

---

**COMMON & PROPER NOUNS**

What is the common noun for the following word?

**Mrs. Smith**

*Proper Noun*

---

**COMMON & PROPER NOUNS**

What is a proper noun for the following word?

**teacher**

*Common Noun*

---

**COMMON & PROPER NOUNS**

What is the common noun for the following word?

**"Red's Adventures"**

*Proper Noun*

---

**COMMON & PROPER NOUNS**

What is a proper noun for the following word?

**TV show**

*Common Noun*

---

**COMMON & PROPER NOUNS**

What is the common noun for the following word?

**Mississippi River**

*Proper Noun*

---

**COMMON & PROPER NOUNS**

What is a proper noun for the following word?

**river**

*Common Noun*

---

*Cooperative Learning & Grammar*
Kagan Publishing • 1 (800) 933-2667 • www.KaganOnline.com

Parts of Speech  **67**

# Parts of Speech
## RallyCoach/Sage-N-Scribe

**Instructions:** Take turns working with your partner to identify the underlined word in each sentence as a noun, verb, adverb, or adjective. Fill in the correct bubble using RallyCoach or Sage-N-Scribe.

### Partner A

Name _____

1. The <u>purple</u> balloon was the birthday girl's favorite.
   - a. noun
   - b. verb
   - c. adverb
   - d. adjective

2. The fish <u>flapped</u> around at the end of the fishing line.
   - a. noun
   - b. verb
   - c. adverb
   - d. adjective

3. My teacher <u>generously</u> gave us a book at the end of the year.
   - a. noun
   - b. verb
   - c. adverb
   - d. adjective

4. I can't wait to see the <u>polar</u> bears at the zoo.
   - a. noun
   - b. verb
   - c. adverb
   - d. adjective

### Partner B

Name _____

1. The runner raced <u>quickly</u> around the last corner to win the marathon.
   - a. noun
   - b. verb
   - c. adverb
   - d. adjective

2. My grandmother cooked a <u>delicious</u> meal of steak and potatoes.
   - a. noun
   - b. verb
   - c. adverb
   - d. adjective

3. The <u>toddler</u> spilled his milk on the floor.
   - a. noun
   - b. verb
   - c. adverb
   - d. adjective

4. The fourth-grader <u>turned</u> his homework in on time everyday.
   - a. noun
   - b. verb
   - c. adverb
   - d. adjective

# Parts of Speech
## RallyCoach/Sage-N-Scribe

**Instructions:** The nouns in the sentence are underlined. First circle the adjective and then put an X over the verb(s). Solve the problems using RallyCoach or Sage-N-Scribe.

### Partner A

Name _____

|  |  |
|---|---|
| 1 | Joe ran up the red stairs. |
| 2 | Sara was swimming in the big pool. |
| 3 | Molly saw a brown bear in the yard. |
| 4 | Anthony walked to the tiny store. |
| 5 | Audrie washed the black dog. |
| 6 | Timothy chewed the disgusting food. |
| 7 | Ms. Kern spoke to the noisy class. |
| 8 | Levi jumped over the tall fence. |
| 9 | The tiger licked his gigantic teeth. |
| 10 | Can you smell the red roses? |
| 11 | Kylie fell off the tall slide. |

### Partner B

Name _____

|  |  |
|---|---|
| 1 | Jill ran up the five steps. |
| 2 | The police officer washed the black uniform. |
| 3 | Jim bought a pink pencil. |
| 4 | Sandy drove to sunny Florida. |
| 5 | Tristin borrowed a purple crayon. |
| 6 | The kids drank ten sodas. |
| 7 | Ryder hit the round baseball. |
| 8 | The green alligator ran into the lake. |
| 9 | The fish ate the fat worm. |
| 10 | Dad grabbed the striped cat. |
| 11 | The little girl was crying. |

**Cooperative Learning & Grammar**
Kagan Publishing • 1 (800) 933-2667 • www.KaganOnline.com

# Parts of Speech
## Find Someone Who

Name _____

**Instructions:** Pair up and take turns identifying the part of speech of the underlined word in each sentence. Write noun, verb, adverb, or adjective in the Parts of Speech box provided. Don't forget your partner's initials.

| # | Sentence | Parts of Speech | Initials |
|---|----------|-----------------|----------|
| 1 | The <u>red</u> and <u>white</u> table cloth was a great place to sit during our picnic. | | |
| 2 | The magician <u>entertained</u> the audience with fascinating tricks. | | |
| 3 | The horse tried <u>hopelessly</u> to jump the corral fence. | | |
| 4 | The principal made an <u>announcement</u> about the upcoming choir concert. | | |
| 5 | The <u>swing set</u> was a popular choice at the state park. | | |
| 6 | The paddle boat began to take on <u>lake</u> water! | | |
| 7 | Our dad <u>cautiously</u> sipped my brother's homemade chicken soup. | | |
| 8 | <u>Ginger</u> sang our national anthem at the football game. | | |
| 9 | I bought <u>fresh</u> fruit at the farmer's market. | | |
| 10 | Gordon <u>received</u> a rocking horse for his birthday. | | |

*Cooperative Learning & Grammar*
Kagan Publishing • 1 (800) 933-2667 • www.KaganOnline.com

# Parts of Speech
## Quiz-Quiz-Trade

**Instructions:** Cut out each card along the dotted line. Then fold each card in half so the question is on one side and the answer is on the back. Glue or tape the cards together to keep the answers and questions on opposite sides.

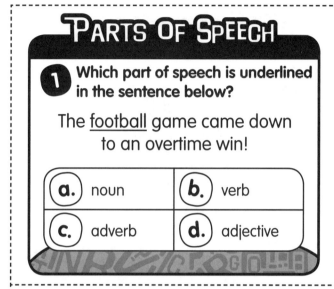

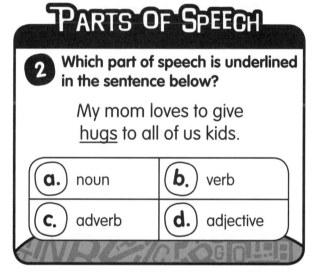

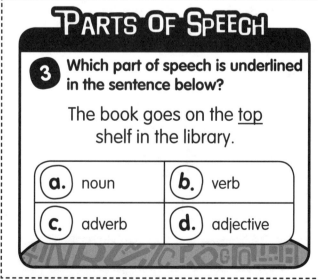

*Cooperative Learning & Grammar*
Kagan Publishing • 1 (800) 933-2667 • www.KaganOnline.com

# PARTS OF SPEECH
## Quiz-Quiz-Trade

**Instructions:** Cut out each card along the dotted line. Then fold each card in half so the question is on one side and the answer is on the back. Glue or tape the cards together to keep the answers and questions on opposite sides.

### PARTS OF SPEECH

**4** Which part of speech is underlined in the sentence below?

Please take a seat <u>quietly</u> and get ready for your spelling test.

a. noun    b. verb
c. adverb  d. adjective

### PARTS OF SPEECH

**5** Which part of speech is underlined in the sentence below?

The motorcycle <u>sped</u> around the dirt track.

a. noun    b. verb
c. adverb  d. adjective

### PARTS OF SPEECH

**6** Which part of speech is underlined in the sentence below?

The young <u>girl</u> wanted a pony for her birthday.

a. noun    b. verb
c. adverb  d. adjective

# Parts of Speech
## Quiz-Quiz-Trade

**Instructions:** Cut out each card along the dotted line. Then fold each card in half so the question is on one side and the answer is on the back. Glue or tape the cards together to keep the answers and questions on opposite sides.

### Parts of Speech

**7.** Which part of speech is underlined in the sentence below?

The <u>treadmill</u> in the gym was a popular spot.

- a. noun
- b. verb
- c. adverb
- d. adjective

### Parts of Speech

**8.** Which part of speech is underlined in the sentence below?

My tennis shoes have a hole in the <u>sole</u>.

- a. noun
- b. verb
- c. adverb
- d. adjective

### Parts of Speech

**9.** Which part of speech is underlined in the sentence below?

Travis <u>drank</u> his chocolate milk through a straw.

- a. noun
- b. verb
- c. adverb
- d. adjective

**Cooperative Learning & Grammar**

# PARTS OF SPEECH
## Quiz-Quiz-Trade

**Instructions:** Cut out each card along the dotted line. Then fold each card in half so the question is on one side and the answer is on the back. Glue or tape the cards together to keep the answers and questions on opposite sides.

### PARTS OF SPEECH

**10** Which part of speech is underlined in the sentence below?

The deer jumped <u>swiftly</u> through the meadow.

- a. noun
- b. verb
- c. adverb
- d. adjective

### PARTS OF SPEECH

**11** Which part of speech is underlined in the sentence below?

The students talk <u>constantly</u> during a lesson.

- a. noun
- b. verb
- c. adverb
- d. adjective

### PARTS OF SPEECH

**12** Which part of speech is underlined in the sentence below?

Can you please <u>drive</u> us to the movies tonight?

- a. noun
- b. verb
- c. adverb
- d. adjective

**Cooperative Learning & Grammar**
Kagan Publishing • 1 (800) 933-2667 • www.KaganOnline.com

# PARTS OF SPEECH
## Quiz-Quiz-Trade

**Instructions:** Cut out each card along the dotted line. Then fold each card in half so the question is on one side and the answer is on the back. Glue or tape the cards together to keep the answers and questions on opposite sides.

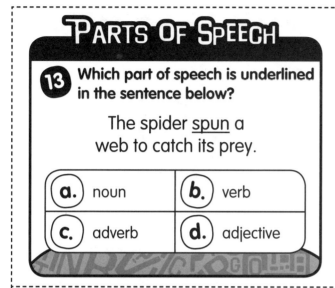

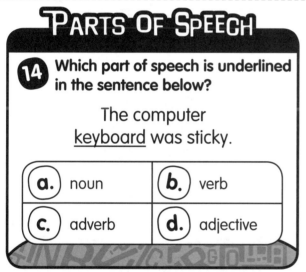

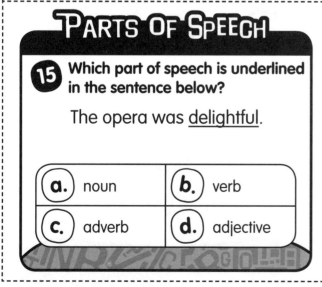

*Cooperative Learning & Grammar*
Kagan Publishing • 1 (800) 933-2667 • www.KaganOnline.com

# Parts of Speech
## Quiz-Quiz-Trade

**Instructions:** Cut out each card along the dotted line. Then fold each card in half so the question is on one side and the answer is on the back. Glue or tape the cards together to keep the answers and questions on opposite sides.

### PARTS OF SPEECH

**16.** Which part of speech is underlined in the sentence below?

The police officer <u>stopped</u> traffic to let children cross the street.

- a. noun
- b. verb
- c. adverb
- d. adjective

### PARTS OF SPEECH

**16.** b. verb

### PARTS OF SPEECH

**17.** Which part of speech is underlined in the sentence below?

The businessman carried his <u>briefcase</u> into the office.

- a. noun
- b. verb
- c. adverb
- d. adjective

### PARTS OF SPEECH

**17.** a. noun

### PARTS OF SPEECH

**18.** Which part of speech is underlined in the sentence below?

The flag flew <u>proudly</u> outside the courthouse.

- a. noun
- b. verb
- c. adverb
- d. adjective

### PARTS OF SPEECH

**18.** c. adverb

Parts of Speech

Cooperative Learning & Grammar
Kagan Publishing • 1 (800) 933-2667 • www.KaganOnline.com

**Instructions:** Cut out each card along the dotted line. Then fold each card in half so the question is on one side and the answer is on the back. Glue or tape the cards together to keep the answers and questions on opposite sides.

## PARTS OF SPEECH

**19** Which part of speech is underlined in the sentence below?

The chameleon <u>changed</u> colors to blend in with his surroundings.

- a. noun
- **b. verb**
- c. adverb
- d. adjective

## PARTS OF SPEECH

**20** Which part of speech is underlined in the sentence below?

The <u>long</u> lighted rope lit up the pathway.

- a. noun
- b. verb
- c. adverb
- **d. adjective**

## PARTS OF SPEECH

**21** Which part of speech is underlined in the sentence below?

The <u>baby</u> cried because she was hungry.

- **a. noun**
- b. verb
- c. adverb
- d. adjective

**Cooperative Learning & Grammar**
Kagan Publishing • 1 (800) 933-2667 • www.KaganOnline.com

# Plural Nouns: Adding -es or -s
### RallyCoach/Sage-N-Scribe

**Instructions:** Take turns working with your partner writing the plural form of the word in the box provided. Solve the problems using RallyCoach or Sage-N-Scribe.

## Partner A

Name _____

| # | Noun | Plural Form |
|---|------|-------------|
| 1 | lunch | |
| 2 | island | |
| 3 | dog | |
| 4 | class | |
| 5 | work | |
| 6 | skate | |
| 7 | helmet | |
| 8 | brush | |
| 9 | branch | |
| 10 | dash | |
| 11 | shirt | |
| 12 | tax | |
| 13 | dress | |
| 14 | club | |

## Partner B

Name _____

| # | Noun | Plural Form |
|---|------|-------------|
| 1 | crunch | |
| 2 | horse | |
| 3 | torch | |
| 4 | house | |
| 5 | fox | |
| 6 | blanket | |
| 7 | box | |
| 8 | hat | |
| 9 | dish | |
| 10 | pouch | |
| 11 | nose | |
| 12 | branch | |
| 13 | nest | |
| 14 | friend | |

# Plural Nouns: Adding -es or -s
## Find Someone Who

Name _____

**Instructions:** Pair up and take turns writing the plural form of each singular noun by adding –es or –s to each word. Don't forget to get your partner's initials.

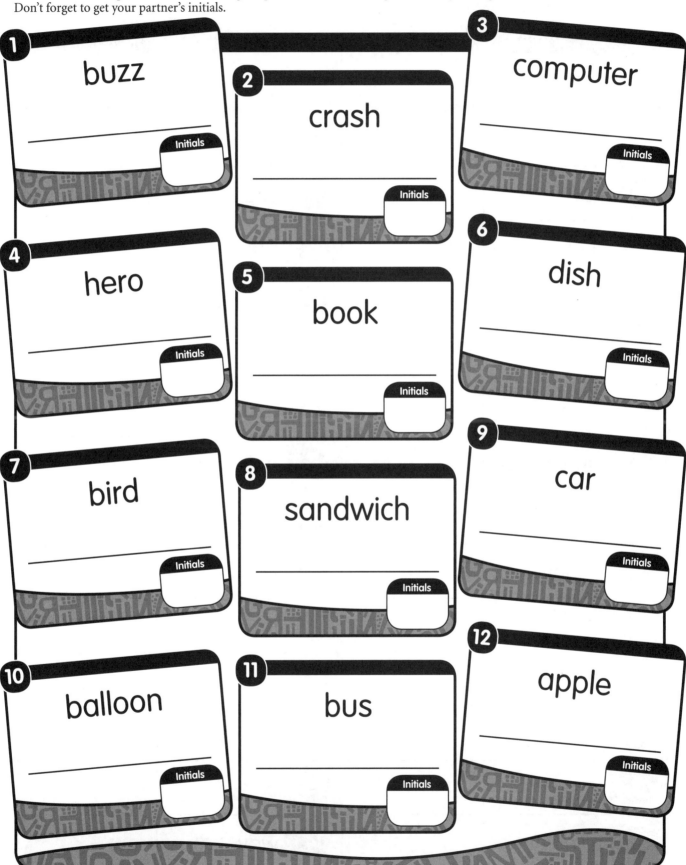

# Plural Nouns: Words Ending in -Y
## RallyCoach/Sage-N-Scribe

**Instructions:** Take turns working with your partner writing the plural form of the word in the box provided. Solve the problems using RallyCoach or Sage-N-Scribe.

### Partner A

Name _____

| # | Noun | Plural Form |
|---|---|---|
| 1 | cherry | |
| 2 | key | |
| 3 | monkey | |
| 4 | story | |
| 5 | baby | |
| 6 | pony | |
| 7 | strawberry | |
| 8 | penny | |
| 9 | guppy | |
| 10 | boy | |
| 11 | chimney | |
| 12 | library | |
| 13 | puppy | |
| 14 | army | |

### Partner B

Name _____

| # | Noun | Plural Form |
|---|---|---|
| 1 | sky | |
| 2 | supply | |
| 3 | party | |
| 4 | attorney | |
| 5 | valley | |
| 6 | company | |
| 7 | hobby | |
| 8 | donkey | |
| 9 | candy | |
| 10 | day | |
| 11 | play | |
| 12 | pantry | |
| 13 | berry | |
| 14 | way | |

# Plural Nouns: Words Ending in -Y
### Find Someone Who

Name _____

**Instructions:** Pair up and take turns writing the plural form of each singular noun. Don't forget to get your partner's initials.

1. city _____ Initials ____
2. penny _____ Initials ____
3. key _____ Initials ____
4. strawberry _____ Initials ____
5. turkey _____ Initials ____
6. guppy _____ Initials ____
7. story _____ Initials ____
8. lady _____ Initials ____
9. toy _____ Initials ____
10. monkey _____ Initials ____
11. chimney _____ Initials ____
12. baby _____ Initials ____

# Plural Nouns: Words Ending in -F or -FE
### RallyCoach/Sage-N-Scribe

**Instructions:** Take turns working with your partner writing the plural form of the word in the box provided. Solve the problems using RallyCoach or Sage-N-Scribe.

## Partner A
Name _____

| # | Noun | Plural Form |
|---|------|-------------|
| 1 | knife | |
| 2 | roof | |
| 3 | calf | |
| 4 | self | |
| 5 | wife | |
| 6 | leaf | |
| 7 | life | |
| 8 | thief | |
| 9 | loaf | |
| 10 | wolf | |

## Partner B
Name _____

| # | Noun | Plural Form |
|---|------|-------------|
| 1 | belief | |
| 2 | dwarf | |
| 3 | shelf | |
| 4 | half | |
| 5 | chief | |
| 6 | bluff | |
| 7 | safe | |
| 8 | staff | |
| 9 | gulf | |
| 10 | brief | |

# Plural Nouns: Words Ending in -F or -FE
## Find Someone Who

Name _____

**Instructions:** Pair up and take turns writing the plural form of each singular noun. Don't forget to get your partner's initials.

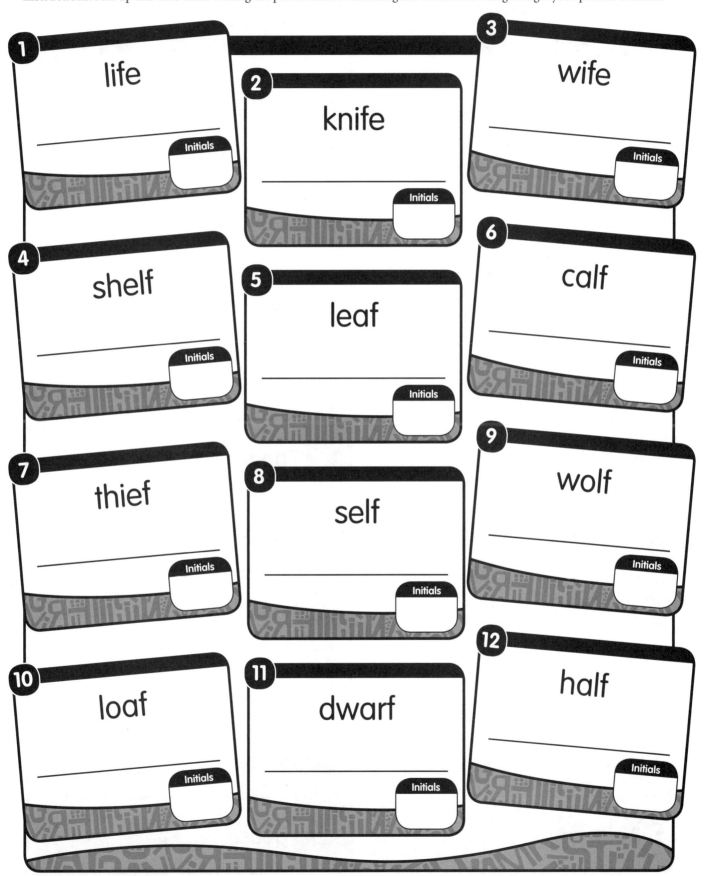

1. life _____ Initials
2. knife _____ Initials
3. wife _____ Initials
4. shelf _____ Initials
5. leaf _____ Initials
6. calf _____ Initials
7. thief _____ Initials
8. self _____ Initials
9. wolf _____ Initials
10. loaf _____ Initials
11. dwarf _____ Initials
12. half _____ Initials

# Irregular Plural Nouns
## RallyCoach/Sage-N-Scribe

**Instructions:** Take turns working with your partner writing the plural form of the word in the box provided. Solve the problems using RallyCoach or Sage-N-Scribe.

### Partner A

Name _____

| Noun | Plural Form |
|---|---|
| 1. ox | |
| 2. tooth | |
| 3. child | |
| 4. foot | |
| 5. deer | |
| 6. octopus | |
| 7. sheep | |
| 8. bus | |
| 9. woman | |
| 10. bison | |

### Partner B

Name _____

| Noun | Plural Form |
|---|---|
| 1. mouse | |
| 2. fish | |
| 3. die | |
| 4. attorney | |
| 5. person | |
| 6. man | |
| 7. medium | |
| 8. swine | |
| 9. louse | |
| 10. goose | |

# Irregular Plural Nouns
## Find Someone Who

Name _____

**Instructions:** Pair up and take turns writing the plural form of each word. Don't forget to get your partner's initials.

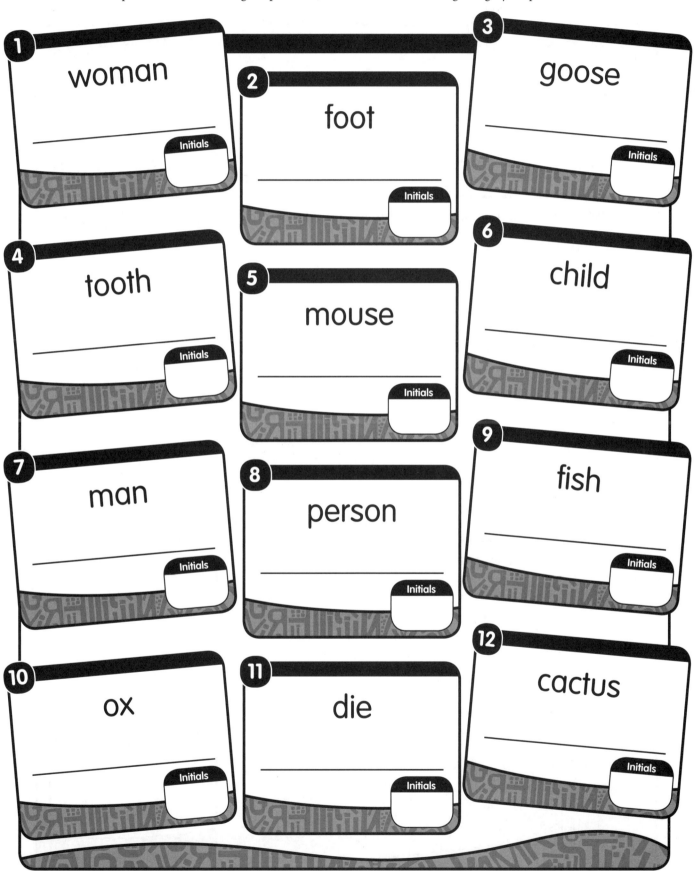

# Plural Nouns: Review
## Find-N-Fix

Name _____

**Instructions:** For each set of problems, find the incorrect plural. Indicate which is incorrect using your Find-N-Fix cards. When your team agrees, fix the incorrect problem.

**1** Which noun is not correctly written in plural form?
1. wifes
2. birds
3. wolves

Fix the Plural Noun
_____

**2** Which noun is not correctly written in plural form?
1. brushes
2. babys
3. halves

Fix the Plural Noun
_____

**3** Which noun is not correctly written in plural form?
1. watches
2. cities
3. shelfs

Fix the Plural Noun
_____

**4** Which noun is not correctly written in plural form?
1. dresses
2. churchs
3. stories

Fix the Plural Noun
_____

**5** Which noun is not correctly written in plural form?
1. butterflys
2. boxes
3. chairs

Fix the Plural Noun
_____

86  Parts of Speech

# Plural Nouns: Review
## Find Someone Who

Name _____

**Instructions:** Pair up and take turns writing the plural form of each singular noun. Don't forget to get your partner's initials.

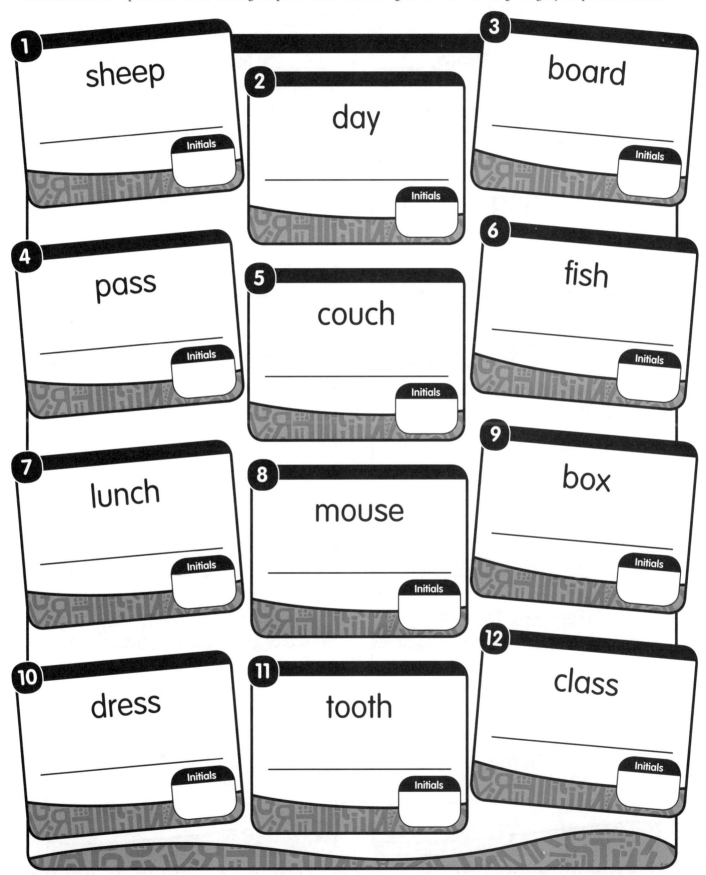

# Plural Nouns Mix-N-Match

**Instructions:** Cut out the cards on the dotted line. Give one card to each student. Distribute cards in sequence so for every student with a Singular Noun card, there is a student with a matching Plural Noun card.

---

**Plural Nouns**

How would you spell this word if there was more than one?

**dog**

Singular Noun

---

**Plural Nouns**

How would you spell this word if there was only one?

**dogs**

Plural Noun

---

**Plural Nouns**

How would you spell this word if there was more than one?

**church**

Singular Noun

---

**Plural Nouns**

How would you spell this word if there was only one?

**churches**

Plural Noun

---

**Plural Nouns**

How would you spell this word if there was more than one?

**wife**

Singular Noun

---

**Plural Nouns**

How would you spell this word if there was only one?

**wives**

Plural Noun

---

88 Parts of Speech

# Plural Nouns Mix-N-Match

**Instructions:** Cut out the cards on the dotted line. Give one card to each student. Distribute cards in sequence so for every student with a Singular Noun card, there is a student with a matching Plural Noun card.

---

### Plural Nouns

How would you spell this word if there was more than one?

**foot**

*Singular Noun*

---

### Plural Nouns

How would you spell this word if there was only one?

**feet**

*Plural Noun*

---

### Plural Nouns

How would you spell this word if there was more than one?

**book**

*Singular Noun*

---

### Plural Nouns

How would you spell this word if there was only one?

**books**

*Plural Noun*

---

### Plural Nouns

How would you spell this word if there was more than one?

**dress**

*Singular Noun*

---

### Plural Nouns

How would you spell this word if there was only one?

**dresses**

*Plural Noun*

---

*Cooperative Learning & Grammar*
Kagan Publishing • 1 (800) 933-2667 • www.KaganOnline.com

# Plural Nouns Mix-N-Match

**Instructions:** Cut out the cards on the dotted line. Give one card to each student. Distribute cards in sequence so for every student with a Singular Noun card, there is a student with a matching Plural Noun card.

---

**PLURAL NOUNS**

How would you spell this word if there was more than one?

**bush**

Singular Noun

---

**PLURAL NOUNS**

How would you spell this word if there was only one?

**bushes**

Plural Noun

---

**PLURAL NOUNS**

How would you spell this word if there was more than one?

**half**

Singular Noun

---

**PLURAL NOUNS**

How would you spell this word if there was only one?

**halves**

Plural Noun

---

**PLURAL NOUNS**

How would you spell this word if there was more than one?

**goose**

Singular Noun

---

**PLURAL NOUNS**

How would you spell this word if there was only one?

**geese**

Plural Noun

# Plural Nouns Mix-N-Match

**Instructions:** Cut out the cards on the dotted line. Give one card to each student. Distribute cards in sequence so for every student with a Singular Noun card, there is a student with a matching Plural Noun card.

---

**PLURAL NOUNS**

How would you spell this word if there was more than one?

**wolf**

*Singular Noun*

---

**PLURAL NOUNS**

How would you spell this word if there was only one?

**wolves**

*Plural Noun*

---

**PLURAL NOUNS**

How would you spell this word if there was more than one?

**pillow**

*Singular Noun*

---

**PLURAL NOUNS**

How would you spell this word if there was only one?

**pillows**

*Plural Noun*

---

**PLURAL NOUNS**

How would you spell this word if there was more than one?

**box**

*Singular Noun*

---

**PLURAL NOUNS**

How would you spell this word if there was only one?

**boxes**

*Plural Noun*

# POSSESSIVE NOUNS
## Find-N-Fix

Name _____

**Instructions:** For each set of problems, find the incorrect sentence. Indicate which is incorrect using your Find-N-Fix cards. When your team agrees, fix the incorrect problem.

**1** In which sentence is the possessive noun incorrect?
1. Our family has six dogs'.
2. The students' desks were all clean.
3. The cat's toy was dirty.

**2** In which sentence is the possessive noun incorrect?
1. All of my friends' parents let them stay up late.
2. The childrens' hands are very dirty.
3. The television's speakers are big and loud.

**3** In which sentence is the possessive noun incorrect?
1. The cell phones' batteries won't last long.
2. The customers' orders have all been filled.
3. I found this baseball in Megans' backyard.

**4** In which sentence is the possessive noun incorrect?
1. Arizonas' mountains have excellent snow for skiing.
2. The paper's surface is excellent for writing poetry.
3. The books' pages are starting to fall out.

**5** In which sentence is the possessive noun incorrect?
1. When the clock's long hand reaches the twelve, we will go to lunch.
2. Omar pulled back the curtains to let the suns' light into the room.
3. The shirt's pocket has a hole in the bottom.

# POSSESSIVE NOUNS
## RallyCoach/Sage-N-Scribe

**Instructions:** Complete each sentence. On the line, write the possessive form of the noun under the line to show belonging. Take turns working with your partner to solve the problems using RallyCoach or Sage-N-Scribe.

## PARTNER A

Name _____

1. This is _____ homework. (Matthew)
2. The _____ pants are black. (boy)
3. That _____ feathers are yellow. (bird)
4. This is _____ jacket. (Sara)
5. The _____ toy is noisy. (dog)
6. My _____ projects are great. (students)
7. Are these _____ quarters? (grandma)
8. The _____ stalls are clean now. (horse)
9. _____ uniform needs to be washed. (Billy)
10. The _____ rattle is blue. (baby)

## PARTNER B

Name _____

1. The _____ milk spilled on the floor. (girl)
2. The _____ handle was hot. (pan)
3. _____ doll has red hair. (Jordon)
4. The _____ ball rolled into the street. (dog)
5. The _____ computer was broken. (woman)
6. The _____ toys were left out in the rain. (children)
7. _____ sister fell off the swing. (Brady)
8. _____ mom brought snacks to school. (Robin)
9. The _____ toy fell on the ground. (cat)
10. The _____ shoes were in his locker. (boy)

*Cooperative Learning & Grammar*

Parts of Speech 93

# POSSESSIVE NOUNS
## Find Someone Who

Name _____

**Instructions:** Pair up and take turns solving one problem on each other's sheet by circling the correct form of the noun to complete the sentence. Don't forget to get your partner's initials.

**1** The **(dog's, dogs')** head.

Initials _____

**2** The **(cat's, cats')** tails.

Initials _____

**3** The **(firefighters', firefighter's)** hoses.

Initials _____

**4** The **(book's, books')** page.

Initials _____

**5** The **(snowman's, snowmans')** nose.

Initials _____

**6** The **(balloon's, balloons')** string is long.

Initials _____

**7** The **(clown's, clowns')** wig made us laugh.

Initials _____

**8** My **(sister's, sisters')** birthday is today.

Initials _____

**9** We saw two **(bear's, bears')** tracks.

Initials _____

94 Parts of Speech

*Cooperative Learning & Grammar*
Kagan Publishing • 1 (800) 933-2667 • www.KaganOnline.com

# POSSESSIVE NOUNS
## Quiz-Quiz-Trade

**Instructions:** Cut out each card along the dotted line. Then fold each card in half so the question is on one side and the answer is on the back. Glue or tape the cards together to keep the answers and questions on opposite sides.

**1. POSSESSIVE NOUNS — Question**
Identify the underlined possessive noun as singular or plural.
The <u>book's</u> pages are wrinkled.

**1. POSSESSIVE NOUNS — Answer**
Singular

**2. POSSESSIVE NOUNS — Question**
Identify the underlined possessive noun as singular or plural.
The <u>girls'</u> ball went over the fence.

**2. POSSESSIVE NOUNS — Answer**
Plural

**3. POSSESSIVE NOUNS — Question**
Identify the underlined possessive noun as singular or plural.
My <u>jacket's</u> button needs to be fixed.

**3. POSSESSIVE NOUNS — Answer**
Singular

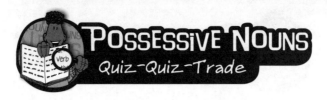

# POSSESSIVE NOUNS
## Quiz-Quiz-Trade

**Instructions:** Cut out each card along the dotted line. Then fold each card in half so the question is on one side and the answer is on the back. Glue or tape the cards together to keep the answers and questions on opposite sides.

### POSSESSIVE NOUNS — 4 — Question
Identify the underlined possessive noun as singular or plural.

The <u>penguins'</u> home is in Antarctica.

### POSSESSIVE NOUNS — 4 — Answer
Plural

### POSSESSIVE NOUNS — 5 — Question
Identify the underlined possessive noun as singular or plural.

The <u>tree's</u> leaves are yellow.

### POSSESSIVE NOUNS — 5 — Answer
Singular

### POSSESSIVE NOUNS — 6 — Question
Identify the underlined possessive noun as singular or plural.

The <u>horses'</u> riders were dressed in red.

### POSSESSIVE NOUNS — 6 — Answer
Plural

*Cooperative Learning & Grammar*
Kagan Publishing • 1 (800) 933-2667 • www.KaganOnline.com

# Possessive Nouns
## Quiz-Quiz-Trade

**Instructions:** Cut out each card along the dotted line. Then fold each card in half so the question is on one side and the answer is on the back. Glue or tape the cards together to keep the answers and questions on opposite sides.

### Possessive Nouns — 7 — Question
Identify the underlined possessive noun as singular or plural.

We can't find the <u>cat's</u> toys.

### Possessive Nouns — 7 — Answer
Singular

### Possessive Nouns — 8 — Question
Identify the underlined possessive noun as singular or plural.

The <u>author's</u> books were very popular.

### Possessive Nouns — 8 — Answer
Singular

### Possessive Nouns — 9 — Question
Identify the underlined possessive noun as singular or plural.

The <u>artists'</u> paintings quickly sold out.

### Possessive Nouns — 9 — Answer
Plural

*Cooperative Learning & Grammar*

# Possessive Nouns
## Quiz-Quiz-Trade

**Instructions:** Cut out each card along the dotted line. Then fold each card in half so the question is on one side and the answer is on the back. Glue or tape the cards together to keep the answers and questions on opposite sides.

**10.** Identify the underlined possessive noun as singular or plural.

Can you see the <u>tiger's</u> paws?

**10.** Singular

**11.** Identify the underlined possessive noun as singular or plural.

The <u>teacher's</u> stapler never works.

**11.** Singular

**12.** Identify the underlined possessive noun as singular or plural.

Can you come to my <u>sister's</u> house?

**12.** Singular

# POSSESSIVE NOUNS
## Quiz-Quiz-Trade

**Instructions:** Cut out each card along the dotted line. Then fold each card in half so the question is on one side and the answer is on the back. Glue or tape the cards together to keep the answers and questions on opposite sides.

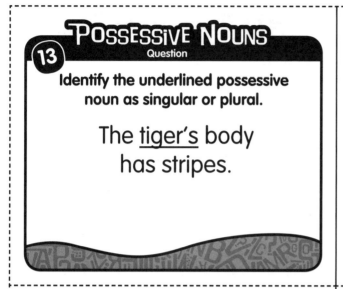

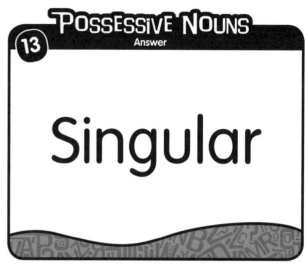

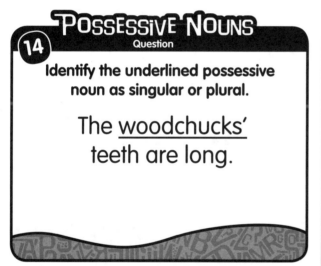

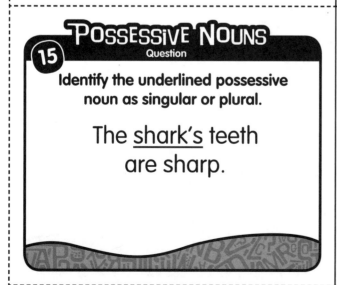

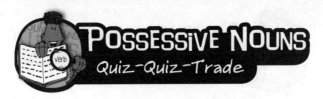

**Instructions:** Cut out each card along the dotted line. Then fold each card in half so the question is on one side and the answer is on the back. Glue or tape the cards together to keep the answers and questions on opposite sides.

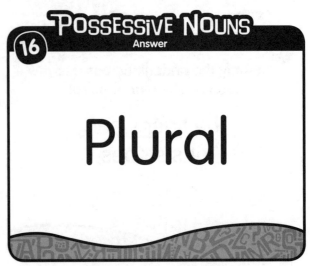

**Instructions:** Cut out each card along the dotted line. Then fold each card in half so the question is on one side and the answer is on the back. Glue or tape the cards together to keep the answers and questions on opposite sides.

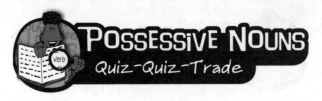

# Possessive Nouns
## Quiz-Quiz-Trade

**Instructions:** Cut out each card along the dotted line. Then fold each card in half so the question is on one side and the answer is on the back. Glue or tape the cards together to keep the answers and questions on opposite sides.

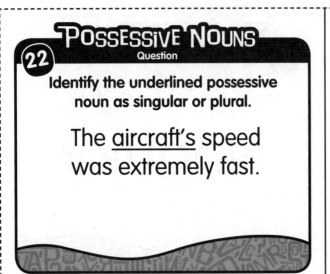

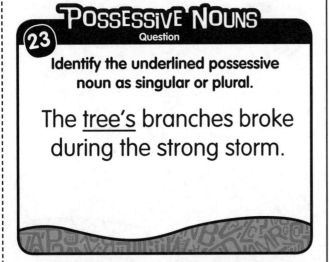

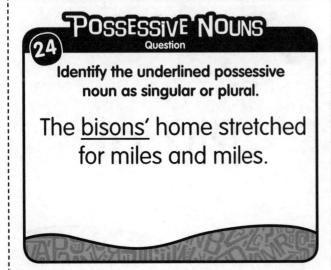

# POSSESSIVE PRONOUNS
## Find Someone Who

Name _____

**Instructions:** Pair up and take turns writing the possessive pronoun on the line. Don't forget to use the information in the parentheses and to get your partner's initials.

**1**
Brush _____ hair.
(The hair belongs to you.)
Initials

**2**
The infant took _____ bottle.
(The bottle belongs to the infant.)
Initials

**3**
_____ guitar lesson is today.
(The guitar lesson is for a boy.)
Initials

**4**
The red bicycle is _____.
(The bicycle belongs to you.)
Initials

**5**
_____ fur was wet.
(The fur belonged to the cat.)
Initials

**6**
_____ tulips are in bloom.
(The tulips belong to me.)
Initials

**7**
The twin boys rode _____ scooters.
(The scooters belonged to the twins.)
Initials

**8**
_____ TV set is broken.
(The TV belongs to us.)
Initials

**9**
The flowers were _____.
(The flowers belonged to a girl.)
Initials

# Pronouns
## RallyCoach/Sage-N-Scribe

**Instructions:** Circle the correct pronoun that best completes the sentence. Take turns working with your partner to using RallyCoach or Sage-N-Scribe to solve the problems.

### Partner A

Name _____

1. Many of **(us, ours)** have studied about Robert E. Lee.
2. **(He, His)** never received a tardy at school.
3. Have **(you, yours)** ever ridden in an airplane?
4. It is clear to **(me, mine)** that Abe Lincoln was a man of honor.
5. **(He, His)** played an important role in our history.
6. Do you think **(she, her)** will be at graduation?
7. **(They, Them)** will be traveling by plane to Hawaii.
8. One man in the parade sang songs for **(we, us)**.
9. **(She, Her)** arrived with them an hour before it was to begin.
10. The shortest stories were **(them, theirs)**.

### Partner B

Name _____

1. **(Our, Ours)** was the best storytime ever.
2. **(You, Yours)** was the funniest story.
3. **(We, Us)** enjoyed the clowns best of all.
4. In the fall, **(they, them)** planted the crops.
5. Soon **(we, us)** will harvest the crops.
6. All day **(it, its)** scares away the birds.
7. **(He, His)** sprayed the garden for insects for my mother.
8. **(I, Me)** tilled the ground on Saturday.
9. We lost **(her, she)** in the line at Funland.
10. The boys and girls cheered for **(them, they)** at the football game.

# PRONOUNS
## Showdown/Fan-N-Pick

**Instructions:** Copy one set of cards for each team. Cut out each card along the dotted line. Give each team a set of cards to play Fan-N-Pick or Showdown.

---

**PRONOUNS**

**1.** What is the pronoun in the sentence below?

You will enjoy traveling by boat.

---

**PRONOUNS**

**2.** What is the pronoun in the sentence below?

Many of us have studied about Abraham Lincoln.

---

**PRONOUNS**

**3.** What is the pronoun in the sentence below?

We will study the Civil War next week.

---

**PRONOUNS**

**4.** What is the pronoun in the sentence below?

I think that is remarkable.

---

**PRONOUNS**

**5.** What is the pronoun in the sentence below?

She didn't know which side of the war was against slavery.

---

**PRONOUNS**

**6.** What is the pronoun in the sentence below?

You can imagine how hard algebra can be.

# PRONOUNS
## Showdown/Fan-N-Pick

**Instructions:** Copy one set of cards for each team. Cut out each card along the dotted line. Give each team a set of cards to play Fan-N-Pick or Showdown.

---

**PRONOUNS**

**7.** What is the pronoun in the sentence below?

Yours was the saddest story.

---

**PRONOUNS**

**8.** What is the pronoun in the sentence below?

She called the police officer.

---

**PRONOUNS**

**9.** What is the pronoun in the sentence below?

He asked Bobby to walk to the park.

---

**PRONOUNS**

**10.** What is the pronoun in the sentence below?

Ours was the best place to see the fireworks.

---

**PRONOUNS**

**11.** What is the pronoun in the sentence below?

Can you boys hear the drums?

---

**PRONOUNS**

**12.** What is the pronoun in the sentence below?

We enjoyed the elephants most of all.

**Instructions:** Copy one set of cards for each team. Cut out each card along the dotted line. Give each team a set of cards to play Fan-N-Pick or Showdown.

---

**PRONOUNS**

**13** Which pronoun best completes the sentence below?

Have **(you, your)** thought about the assignment?

---

**PRONOUNS**

**14** Which pronoun best completes the sentence below?

Sue and **(she, her)** went to the mall.

---

**PRONOUNS**

**15** Which pronoun best completes the sentence below?

Which of **(we, you)** will be elected?

---

**PRONOUNS**

**16** Which pronoun best completes the sentence below?

**(He, Him)** asked us to walk faster.

---

**PRONOUNS**

**17** Which pronoun best completes the sentence below?

George wanted an education, which would help **(him, his)** future.

---

**PRONOUNS**

**18** Which pronoun best completes the sentence below?

How will **(them, they)** get to the other side?

---

*Cooperative Learning & Grammar*

# PRONOUNS
## Quiz-Quiz-Trade

**Instructions:** Cut out each card along the dotted line. Then fold each card in half so the question is on one side and the answer is on the back. Glue or tape the cards together to keep the answers and questions on opposite sides.

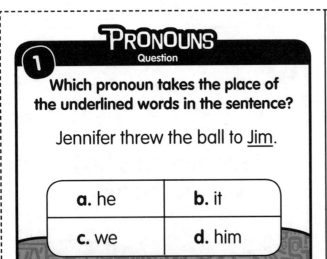

**1** — **PRONOUNS** Question

Which pronoun takes the place of the underlined words in the sentence?

Jennifer threw the ball to <u>Jim</u>.

| a. he | b. it |
|---|---|
| c. we | d. him |

**1** — **PRONOUNS** Answer

d. him

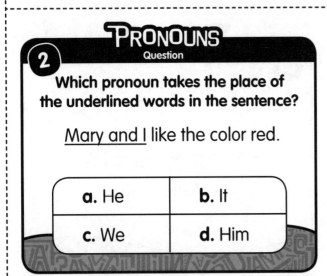

**2** — **PRONOUNS** Question

Which pronoun takes the place of the underlined words in the sentence?

<u>Mary and I</u> like the color red.

| a. He | b. It |
|---|---|
| c. We | d. Him |

**2** — **PRONOUNS** Answer

c. We

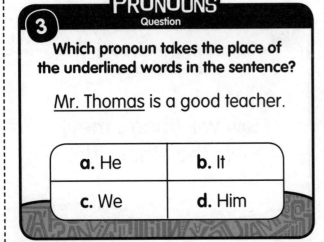

**3** — **PRONOUNS** Question

Which pronoun takes the place of the underlined words in the sentence?

<u>Mr. Thomas</u> is a good teacher.

| a. He | b. It |
|---|---|
| c. We | d. Him |

**3** — **PRONOUNS** Answer

a. He

**Instructions:** Cut out each card along the dotted line. Then fold each card in half so the question is on one side and the answer is on the back. Glue or tape the cards together to keep the answers and questions on opposite sides.

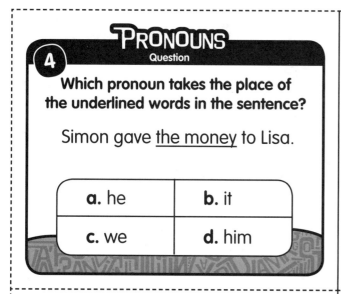

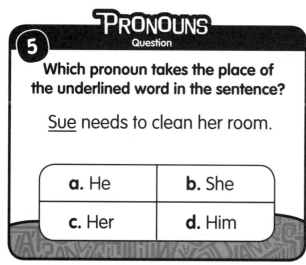
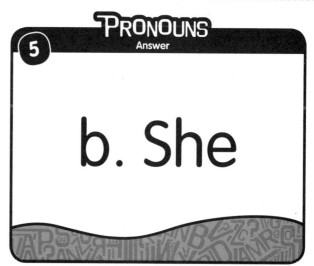
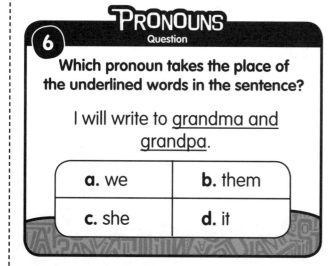

**Cooperative Learning & Grammar**

# PRONOUNS
## Quiz-Quiz-Trade

**Instructions:** Cut out each card along the dotted line. Then fold each card in half so the question is on one side and the answer is on the back. Glue or tape the cards together to keep the answers and questions on opposite sides.

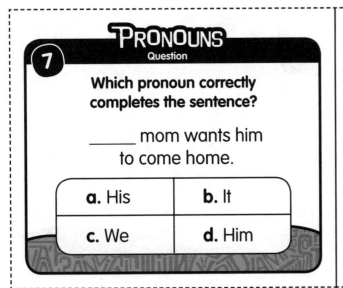

**7** — Which pronoun correctly completes the sentence?

_____ mom wants him to come home.

| a. His | b. It |
| c. We | d. Him |

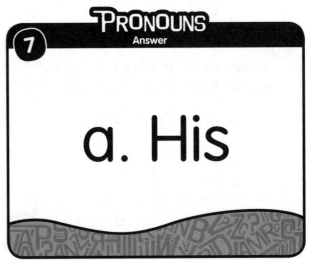

**7** — a. His

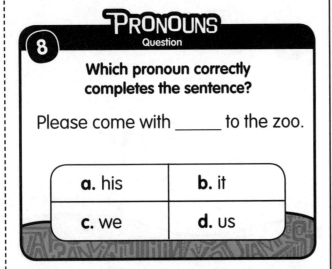

**8** — Which pronoun correctly completes the sentence?

Please come with _____ to the zoo.

| a. his | b. it |
| c. we | d. us |

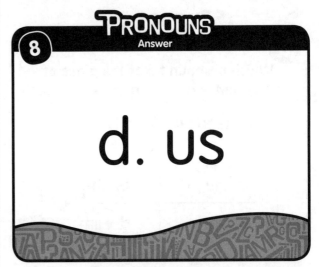

**8** — d. us

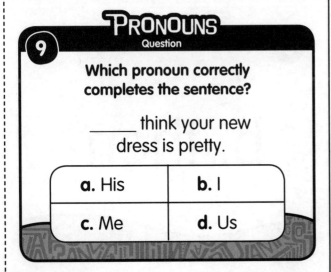

**9** — Which pronoun correctly completes the sentence?

_____ think your new dress is pretty.

| a. His | b. I |
| c. Me | d. Us |

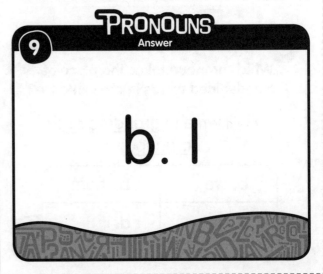

**9** — b. I

110 Parts of Speech

Cooperative Learning & Grammar
Kagan Publishing • 1 (800) 933-2667 • www.KaganOnline.com

# PRONOUNS
## Quiz-Quiz-Trade

**Instructions:** Cut out each card along the dotted line. Then fold each card in half so the question is on one side and the answer is on the back. Glue or tape the cards together to keep the answers and questions on opposite sides.

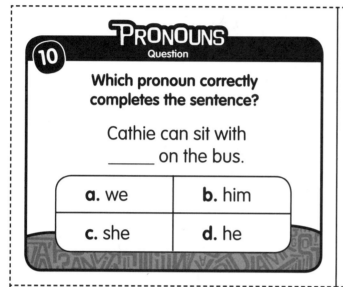

**10** — Which pronoun correctly completes the sentence?

Cathie can sit with _____ on the bus.

| a. we | b. him |
| c. she | d. he |

**10** — b. him

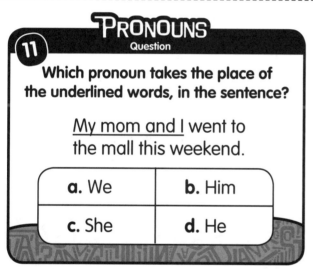

**11** — Which pronoun takes the place of the underlined words, in the sentence?

<u>My mom and I</u> went to the mall this weekend.

| a. We | b. Him |
| c. She | d. He |

**11** — a. We

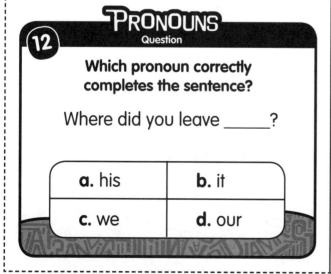

**12** — Which pronoun correctly completes the sentence?

Where did you leave _____?

| a. his | b. it |
| c. we | d. our |

**12** — b. it

*Cooperative Learning & Grammar*
Kagan Publishing • 1 (800) 933-2667 • www.KaganOnline.com

Parts of Speech 111

**Instructions:** Cut out each card along the dotted line. Then fold each card in half so the question is on one side and the answer is on the back. Glue or tape the cards together to keep the answers and questions on opposite sides.

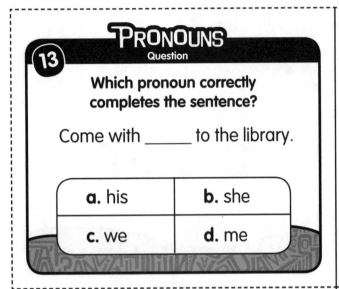
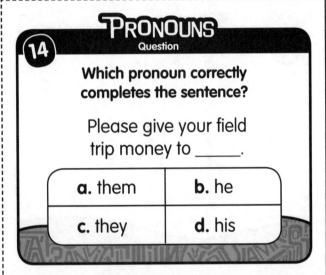
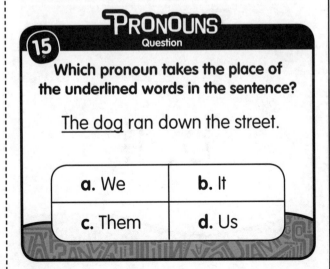

112  Parts of Speech

Cooperative Learning & Grammar
Kagan Publishing • 1 (800) 933-2667 • www.KaganOnline.com

# PRONOUNS
## Quiz-Quiz-Trade

**Instructions:** Cut out each card along the dotted line. Then fold each card in half so the question is on one side and the answer is on the back. Glue or tape the cards together to keep the answers and questions on opposite sides.

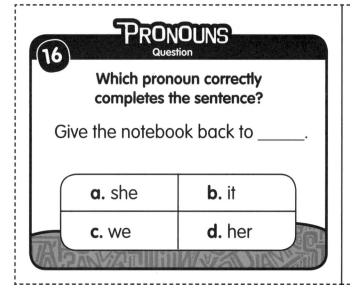
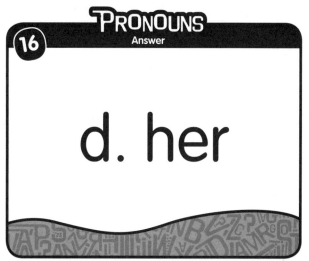
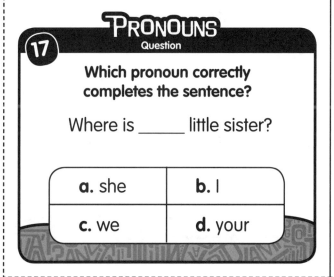
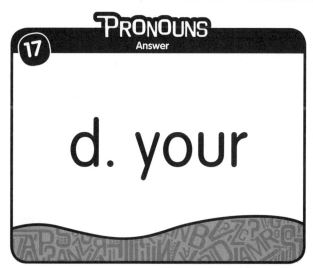
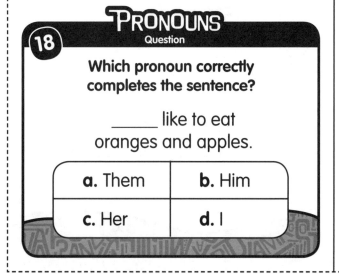
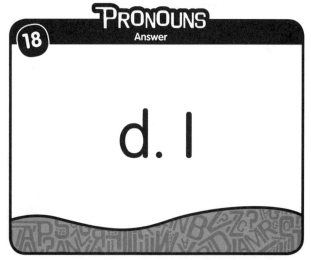

# PRONOUNS
## Quiz-Quiz-Trade

**Instructions:** Cut out each card along the dotted line. Then fold each card in half so the question is on one side and the answer is on the back. Glue or tape the cards together to keep the answers and questions on opposite sides.

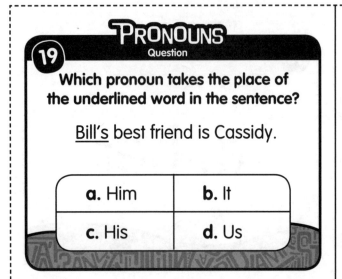
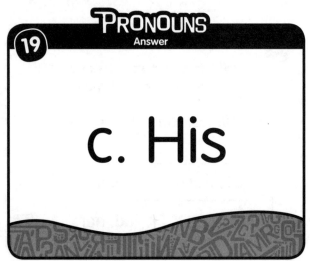
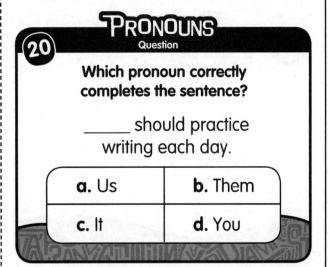
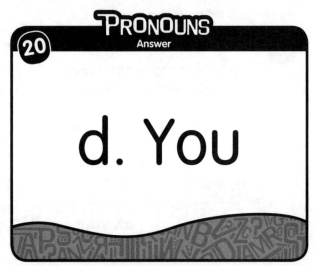
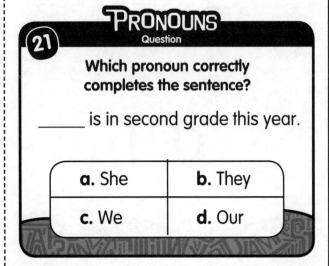

114  Parts of Speech

# Suffixes
## RallyCoach/Sage-N-Scribe

**Instructions:** In the sentences below use the suffix, *-er*, *-ful*, or *-less*, to make a new word for the underlined word in the box provided. Take turns working with your partner to solve the problems using RallyCoach or Sage-N-Scribe.

### Partner A

Name _____

| # | Word | Word with Suffix |
|---|------|------------------|
| 1 | full of wonder | |
| 2 | without care | |
| 3 | one who can bake | |
| 4 | full of cheer | |
| 5 | without worth | |
| 6 | one who can read | |
| 7 | full of meaning | |

### Partner B

Name _____

| # | Word | Word with Suffix |
|---|------|------------------|
| 1 | one who can garden | |
| 2 | full of success | |
| 3 | one who can paint | |
| 4 | full of skill | |
| 5 | without a child | |
| 6 | one who can jump | |
| 7 | without a clue | |

# Suffixes & Prefixes
## Find Someone Who

Name _____

**Instructions:** Pair up and take turns using the prefixes and suffixes in the bank to add to the root words below. Write the meaning of the new word on the line. Don't forget to get your partner's initials.

### Suffixes & Prefixes Bank

un-   re-   -ful   -er   in-   -less   pre-

1. ☐ lock — Definition _____ Initials ____
2. fright ☐ — Definition _____ Initials ____
3. ☐ comfortable — Definition _____ Initials ____
4. pain ☐ — Definition _____ Initials ____
5. ☐ school — Definition _____ Initials ____
6. report ☐ — Definition _____ Initials ____
7. ☐ wind — Definition _____ Initials ____
8. care ☐ — Definition _____ Initials ____
9. color ☐ — Definition _____ Initials ____

**Name** _____

**Instructions:** Pair up and take turns finding the word in the sentence with a prefix or suffix. Circle the root word and underline the prefix or suffix. Don't forget to get your partner's initials.

| 1 | 2 | 3 |
|---|---|---|
| I need to preheat the oven. | Please rewind the movie. | We closely watched the pot boil. |
| Initials: | Initials: | Initials: |
| **4** | **5** | **6** |
| What a beautiful butterfly! | Please speak into the microphone. | Molly found the largest frog in the pond. |
| Initials: | Initials: | Initials: |
| **7** | **8** | **9** |
| I saw my preschool teacher at the grocery store. | The vacuum has many attachments. | Daniel is the fastest runner in our class. |
| Initials: | Initials: | Initials: |

# Prefix, Suffix & Root Words
## Quiz-Quiz-Trade

**Instructions:** Cut out each card along the dotted line. Then fold each card in half so the question is on one side and the answer is on the back. Glue or tape the cards together to keep the answers and questions on opposite sides.

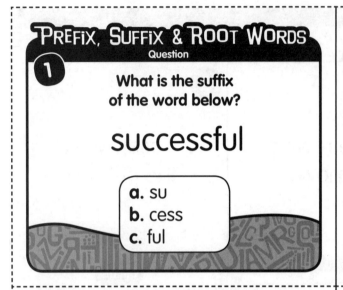

**1** What is the suffix of the word below?

successful

a. su
b. cess
c. ful

**1** c. ful

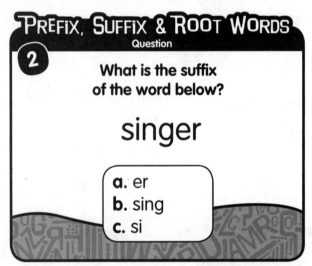

**2** What is the suffix of the word below?

singer

a. er
b. sing
c. si

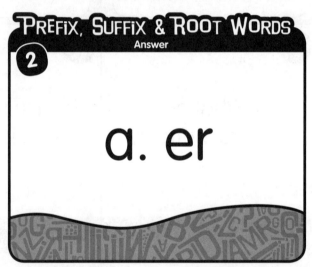

**2** a. er

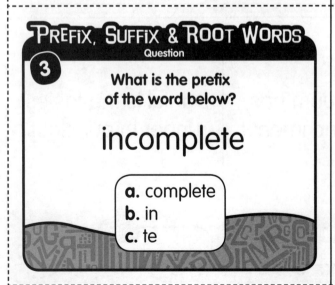

**3** What is the prefix of the word below?

incomplete

a. complete
b. in
c. te

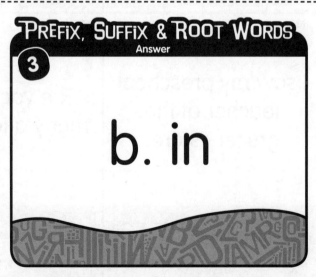

**3** b. in

# Prefix, Suffix & Root Words
## Quiz-Quiz-Trade

**Instructions:** Cut out each card along the dotted line. Then fold each card in half so the question is on one side and the answer is on the back. Glue or tape the cards together to keep the answers and questions on opposite sides.

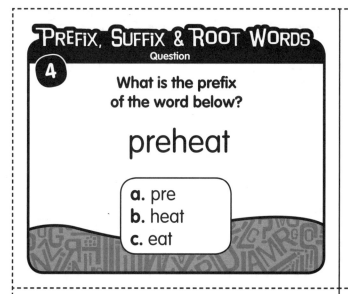

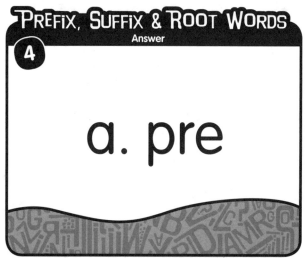

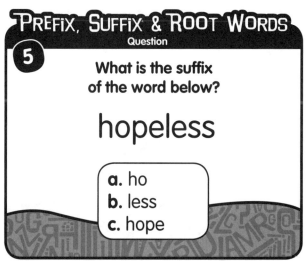

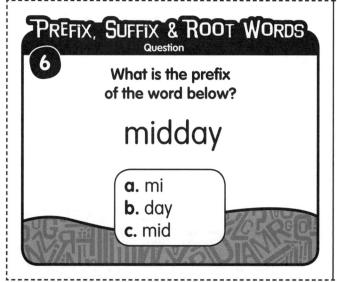

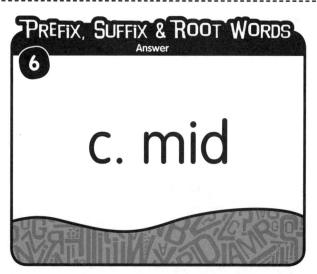

*Cooperative Learning & Grammar*

# Prefix, Suffix & Root Words
## Quiz-Quiz-Trade

**Instructions:** Cut out each card along the dotted line. Then fold each card in half so the question is on one side and the answer is on the back. Glue or tape the cards together to keep the answers and questions on opposite sides.

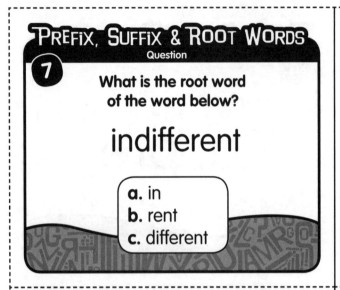
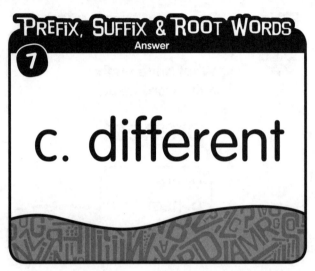
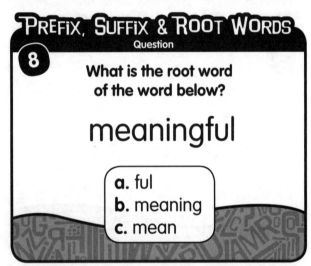
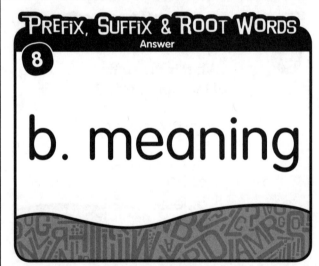
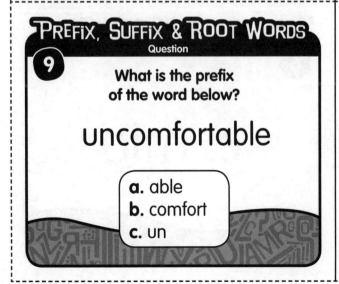
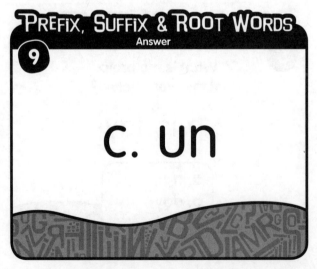

120 Parts of Speech

Cooperative Learning & Grammar
Kagan Publishing • 1 (800) 933-2667 • www.KaganOnline.com

# Prefix, Suffix & Root Words
## Quiz-Quiz-Trade

**Instructions:** Cut out each card along the dotted line. Then fold each card in half so the question is on one side and the answer is on the back. Glue or tape the cards together to keep the answers and questions on opposite sides.

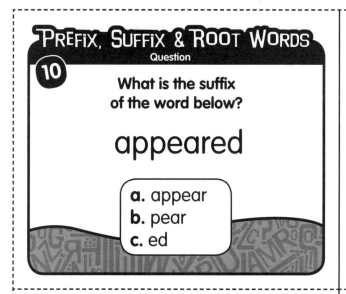

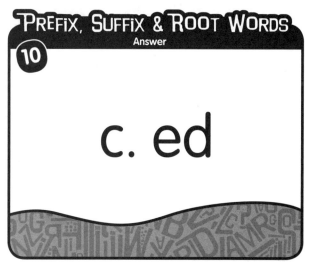

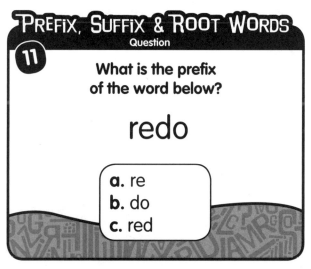

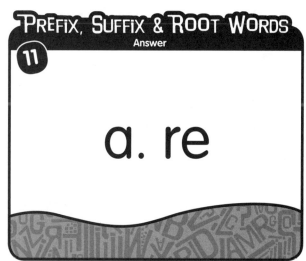

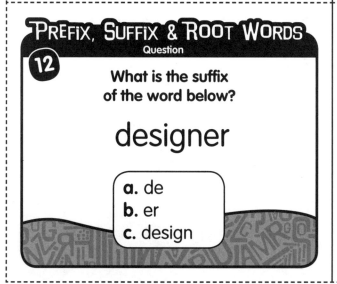

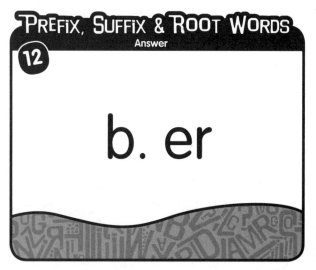

*Cooperative Learning & Grammar*

# Prefix, Suffix & Root Words
## Quiz-Quiz-Trade

**Instructions:** Cut out each card along the dotted line. Then fold each card in half so the question is on one side and the answer is on the back. Glue or tape the cards together to keep the answers and questions on opposite sides.

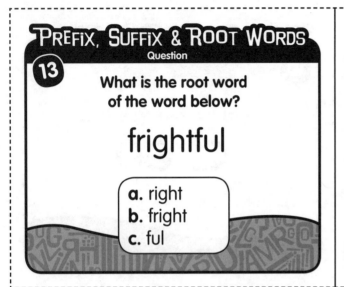

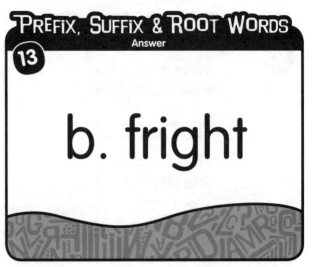

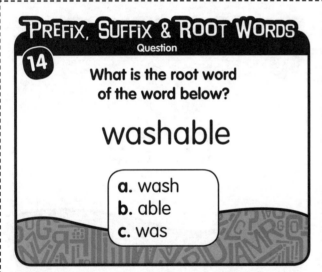

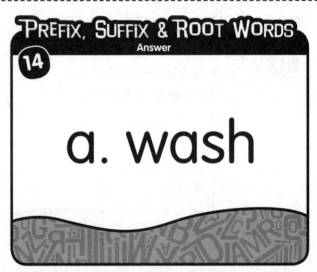

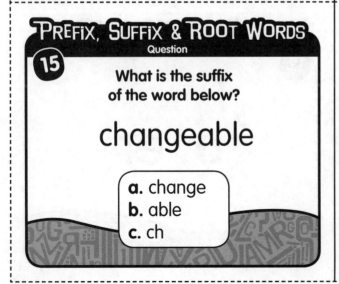

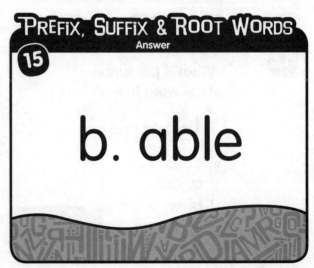

# Prefix, Suffix & Root Words
## Quiz-Quiz-Trade

**Instructions:** Cut out each card along the dotted line. Then fold each card in half so the question is on one side and the answer is on the back. Glue or tape the cards together to keep the answers and questions on opposite sides.

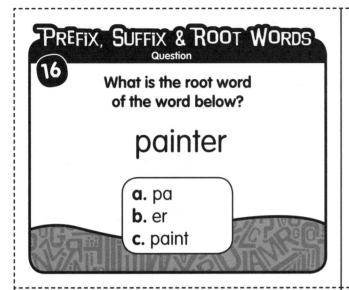
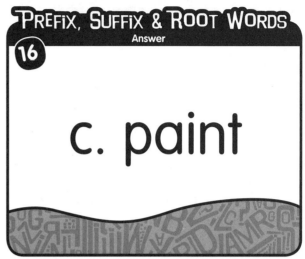
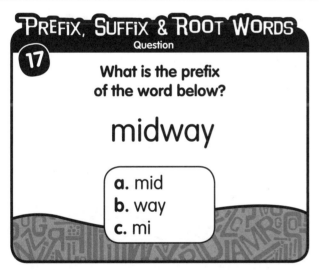

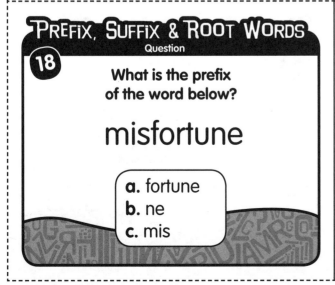

Cooperative Learning & Grammar

# Prefix, Suffix & Root Words
## Quiz-Quiz-Trade

**Instructions:** Cut out each card along the dotted line. Then fold each card in half so the question is on one side and the answer is on the back. Glue or tape the cards together to keep the answers and questions on opposite sides.

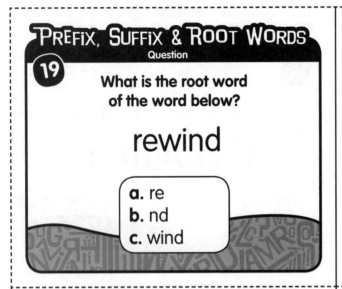

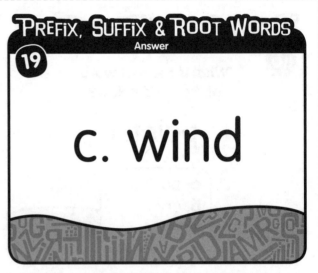

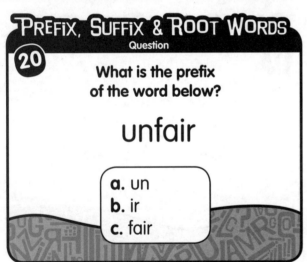

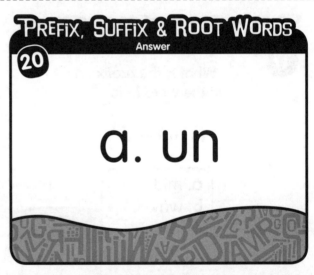

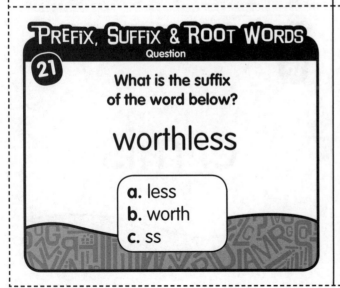

**Instructions:** Cut out each card along the dotted line. Then fold each card in half so the question is on one side and the answer is on the back. Glue or tape the cards together to keep the answers and questions on opposite sides.

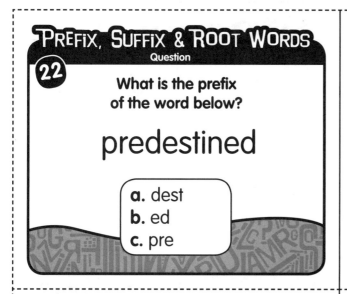
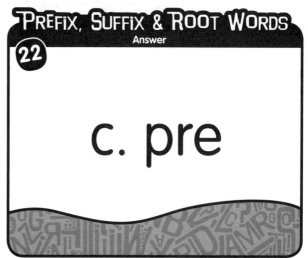
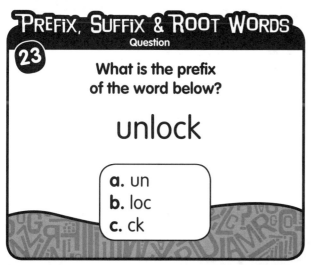

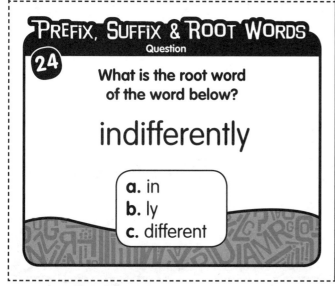
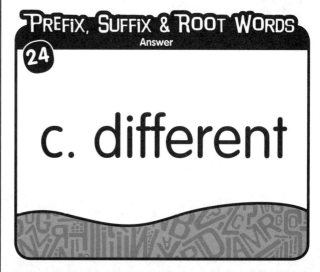

# Articles Find-N-Fix

Name _____

**Instructions:** For each set of problems, find the incorrect sentence. Indicate which is incorrect using your Find-N-Fix cards. When your team agrees, fix the incorrect problem.

**1** Which sentence does not use the articles a/an correctly?
1. Susie chose an piece of apple pie.
2. We went to a movie last night.
3. We built a campfire last night.

**2** Which sentence does not use the articles a/an correctly?
1. We took an English test.
2. He was a officer in the Army.
3. They saw a deer on their trip.

**3** Which sentence does not use the articles a/an correctly?
1. Mark has a orange and brown sweater.
2. We had a cookie and an ice-cream cone.
3. I got an outfield hit in the big game.

**4** Which sentence does not use the articles a/an correctly?
1. A honest friend is someone to respect.
2. Meg had a piano lesson after school.
3. My family went to a play in New York.

**5** Which sentence does not use the articles a/an correctly?
1. Emily bought a new pair of skates.
2. Ned has an old bicycle.
3. Carmen thought the car was a ugly color.

126  Parts of Speech

Cooperative Learning & Grammar
Kagan Publishing • 1 (800) 933-2667 • www.KaganOnline.com

# Articles
## RallyCoach/Sage-N-Scribe

**Instructions:** Take turns working with your partner to circle either "a" or "an" to correctly complete each sentence. Use RallyCoach or Sage-N-Scribe to solve the problems.

## Partner A

Name _____

1. Missy wanted (a, an) dog for her birthday.
2. The TV had (a, an) scratch on the screen and made it difficult to watch.
3. Jacob ate (a, an) apple at lunch.
4. Kelly has (a, an) art project to work on after school.
5. The monkey climbing in the tree had (a, an) banana in his hand.
6. Michael wanted to ride his bike so his mom said to wear (a, an) helmet.
7. During the school play, the choir sang (a, an) song about sharing.
8. In dance class, we are learning (a, an) Indian dance for our recital.
9. I wanted to wear (a, an) orange shirt for the class pictures.
10. Carrie wanted to go swimming with (a, an) dolphin in the ocean.
11. Shelly saw (a, an) elephant on her visit to the zoo.

## Partner B

Name _____

1. Papa caught (a, an) fish at the lake.
2. Michelle wanted to go to (a, an) movie at the local theater.
3. Gordon visited (a, an) enormous house on his vacation.
4. Lynn's mom said she could eat (a, an) ice-cream cone for desert.
5. The blanket had (a, an) stain on it from the mud.
6. Aaron went to the store to buy (a, an) airplane for his collection.
7. The turtle was hiding in his shell from (a, an) car that passed by him on the road.
8. The spider spun (a, an) web high in the tree branches.
9. We were told to use (a, an) exit door in case of an emergency.
10. Clint had (a, an) old bicycle that needed to be fixed.
11. The magazine wanted (a, an) picture of babies for their next issue.

**Cooperative Learning & Grammar**

# COMPOUND WORDS
## RallyCoach/Sage-N-Scribe

**Instructions:** Add one word to each group of words to form a compound word with each of the words in the group. Take turns working with your partner using RallyCoach or Sage-N-Scribe to solve the problems.

## Partner A

Name _____

1. her, him, your _____
2. fire, mail, milk _____
3. every, any, no _____
4. ear, back, head _____
5. school, class, bed _____
6. to, Sun, birth _____
7. card, chalk, back _____

## Partner B

Name _____

1. sail, speed, motor _____
2. drive, free, high _____
3. in, be, out _____
4. pocket, cook, note _____
5. base, snow, basket _____
6. flash, stop, day _____
7. half, quarter, running _____

128 Parts of Speech

# COMPOUND WORDS
## Find Someone Who

Name _____

**Instructions:** Pair up and take turns solving one problem on each other's sheet. Don't forget to get your partner's initials.

---

**1** Which word below is a compound word?
- a. rainbow
- b. evening
- c. grill
- d. soccer

Initials: _____

**2** Find the word that forms a compound word.

mail_____
- a. road
- b. box
- c. dog

Initials: _____

**3** Which word below is a compound word?
- a. swimming
- b. computer
- c. baseball
- d. dresser

Initials: _____

**4** Find the word that forms a compound word.

dog_____
- a. house
- b. toy
- c. treat

Initials: _____

**5** Fill in the lines below to form compound words.

dog_____
air_____
bath_____

Initials: _____

**6** Which word below is a compound word?
- a. preheat
- b. rewind
- c. deck
- d. bedtime

Initials: _____

**7** Find the word that forms a compound word.

sun_____
- a. shine
- b. bow
- c. rain

Initials: _____

**8** Which word below is a compound word?
- a. touchdown
- b. video
- c. flower
- d. sugar

Initials: _____

**9** Fill in the lines below to form compound words.

snow_____
_____dog
straw_____

Initials: _____

# COMPOUND WORDS
## Mix-N-Match

**Instructions:** Cut out the cards on the dotted line. Give one card to each student. Distribute cards in sequence so for every student with a Word card, there is a student with a matching Word card to form a compound word.

### COMPOUND WORDS
What word could you add to this word to make a compound word?

mail_____

### COMPOUND WORDS
What word could you add to this word to make a compound word?

_____box

### COMPOUND WORDS
What word could you add to this word to make a compound word?

sun_____

### COMPOUND WORDS
What word could you add to this word to make a compound word?

_____flower

### COMPOUND WORDS
What word could you add to this word to make a compound word?

dog_____

### COMPOUND WORDS
What word could you add to this word to make a compound word?

_____house

# COMPOUND WORDS
## Mix-N-Match

**Instructions:** Cut out the cards on the dotted line. Give one card to each student. Distribute cards in sequence so for every student with a Word card, there is a student with a matching Word card to form a compound word.

---

### COMPOUND WORDS

What word could you add to this word to make a compound word?

light_____

---

### COMPOUND WORDS

What word could you add to this word to make a compound word?

_____bulb

---

### COMPOUND WORDS

What word could you add to this word to make a compound word?

air_____

---

### COMPOUND WORDS

What word could you add to this word to make a compound word?

_____port

---

### COMPOUND WORDS

What word could you add to this word to make a compound word?

basket_____

---

### COMPOUND WORDS

What word could you add to this word to make a compound word?

_____ball

# COMPOUND WORDS
## Mix-N-Match

**Instructions:** Cut out the cards on the dotted line. Give one card to each student. Distribute cards in sequence so for every student with a Word card, there is a student with a matching Word card to form a compound word.

---

**COMPOUND WORDS**

What word could you add to this word to make a compound word?

door_____

---

**COMPOUND WORDS**

What word could you add to this word to make a compound word?

_____knob

---

**COMPOUND WORDS**

What word could you add to this word to make a compound word?

flash_____

---

**COMPOUND WORDS**

What word could you add to this word to make a compound word?

_____light

---

**COMPOUND WORDS**

What word could you add to this word to make a compound word?

grass_____

---

**COMPOUND WORDS**

What word could you add to this word to make a compound word?

_____hopper

# COMPOUND WORDS
## Mix-N-Match

**Instructions:** Cut out the cards on the dotted line. Give one card to each student. Distribute cards in sequence so for every student with a Word card, there is a student with a matching Word card to form a compound word.

---

### COMPOUND WORDS

What word could you add to this word to make a compound word?

hair_____

---

### COMPOUND WORDS

What word could you add to this word to make a compound word?

_____cut

---

### COMPOUND WORDS

What word could you add to this word to make a compound word?

rail_____

---

### COMPOUND WORDS

What word could you add to this word to make a compound word?

_____road

---

### COMPOUND WORDS

What word could you add to this word to make a compound word?

stop_____

---

### COMPOUND WORDS

What word could you add to this word to make a compound word?

_____watch

---

*Cooperative Learning & Grammar*
Kagan Publishing • 1 (800) 933-2667 • www.KaganOnline.com

# CONTRACTIONS
## Find-N-Fix

Name _____

**Instructions:** For each set of problems, find the incorrect contraction. Indicate which is incorrect using your Find-N-Fix cards. When your team agrees, fix the incorrect problem.

**1** Which of the following contractions is written incorrectly?
1. does'nt
2. can't
3. she's

**Fix the Contraction**

**2** Which of the following contractions is written incorrectly?
1. isn't
2. wo'nt
3. she'll

**Fix the Contraction**

**3** Which of the following contractions is written incorrectly?
1. couldn't
2. it's
3. wel'l

**Fix the Contraction**

**4** Which of the following contractions is written incorrectly?
1. he's
2. woul'dnt
3. I'm

**Fix the Contraction**

**5** Which of the following contractions is written incorrectly?
1. Iv'e
2. shouldn't
3. don't

**Fix the Contraction**

# CONTRACTIONS
## RallyCoach/Sage-N-Scribe

**Instructions:** Take turns working with your partner to choose the contraction that will complete the sentence correctly using RallyCoach or Sage-N-Scribe to solve the problems.

## Partner A

Name _____

**1.** My sister and I _____ done our evening chores.
- a. didn't
- b. won't
- c. haven't
- d. we'll

**2.** We _____ planning to attend the school dance tonight.
- a. aren't
- b. ain't
- c. won't
- d. isn't

**3.** Do you think _____ coming to the game?
- a. isn't
- b. they're
- c. he'll
- d. she'd

**4.** Jacob and Cassidy _____ follow the directions.
- a. they'd
- b. isn't
- c. didn't
- d. here's

## Partner B

Name _____

**1.** Kelly _____ have to fold the laundry by herself.
- a. we'll
- b. haven't
- c. she'll
- d. shouldn't

**2.** _____ going to be late to the party.
- a. She'd
- b. He's
- c. Isn't
- d. Won't

**3.** I _____ carry all of these books by myself.
- a. haven't
- b. can't
- c. wasn't
- d. she'd

**4.** Rebecca _____ be able to go swimming with us today.
- a. won't
- b. isn't
- c. haven't
- d. she'd

# CONTRACTIONS
## RallyCoach/Sage-N-Scribe

**Instructions:** Take turns working with your partner to write the two words that form each contraction using RallyCoach or Sage-N-Scribe to solve the problems.

## Partner A

Name _____

1. wouldn't _____
2. they're _____
3. we've _____
4. there's _____
5. he'll _____
6. couldn't _____
7. don't _____
8. doesn't _____
9. you've _____
10. it's _____
11. shouldn't _____
12. we're _____
13. hasn't _____

## Partner B

Name _____

1. that's _____
2. here's _____
3. we'd _____
4. I've _____
5. aren't _____
6. we're _____
7. you've _____
8. didn't _____
9. hasn't _____
10. she's _____
11. I'd _____
12. he'd _____
13. weren't _____

# CONTRACTIONS
## RallyCoach/Sage-N-Scribe

**Instructions:** Take turns working with your partner to write the contraction for each pair of words using RallyCoach or Sage-N-Scribe to solve the problems.

## Partner A

Name _____

1. she is _____
2. does not _____
3. we would _____
4. you have _____
5. do not _____
6. they would _____
7. were not _____
8. that is _____
9. would not _____
10. I am _____
11. was not _____
12. you will _____
13. there is _____

## Partner B

Name _____

1. is not _____
2. we will _____
3. was not _____
4. you are _____
5. you would _____
6. we will _____
7. they are _____
8. I have _____
9. it is _____
10. you have _____
11. are not _____
12. he would _____
13. she will _____

Parts of Speech 137

# CONTRACTIONS
## RallyCoach/Sage-N-Scribe

**Instructions:** Take turns working with your partner to write the two words that form each contraction or the contraction from each pair of words. Use RallyCoach or Sage-N-Scribe to solve the problems.

## Partner A

Name _____

### Write the pair of words that make up each contraction.

1. she'll _____
2. wouldn't _____
3. I've _____
4. you're _____
5. they've _____

### Write the contraction from each pair of words.

6. it + is _____
7. what + is _____
8. I + would _____
9. here + is _____
10. we + have _____

## Partner B

Name _____

### Write the pair of words that make up each contraction.

1. didn't _____
2. they're _____
3. she's _____
4. they'd _____
5. he'll _____

### Write the contraction from each pair of words.

6. who + is _____
7. is + not _____
8. could + not _____
9. I + have _____
10. he + is _____

Name _____

**Instructions:** Pair up and take turns writing the two words that form each contraction. Don't forget to get your partner's initials.

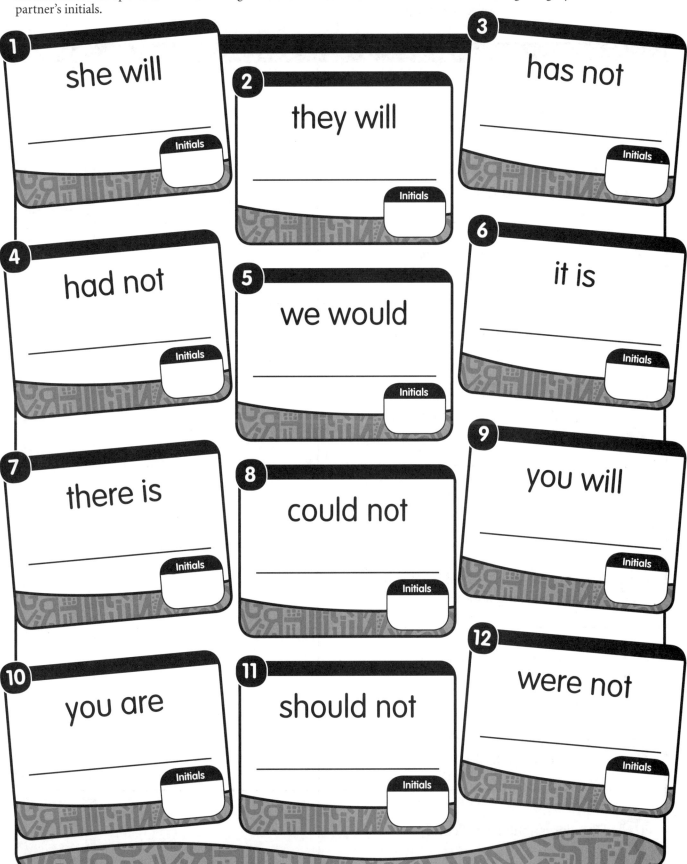

# CONTRACTIONS
## Find Someone Who

**Name** _____

**Instructions:** Pair up and take turns circling the contraction in each sentence. Write the pair of words each contraction stands for in the box provided. Don't forget your partner's initials.

| | Sentence | Contraction Word Pair | Initials |
|---|---|---|---|
| 1 | I'll get our lunches and bring them to the table. | | |
| 2 | We won't be able to make the party because we have homework to do. | | |
| 3 | Why couldn't we read the whole book before we watched the movie? | | |
| 4 | Here's the lost map for our hidden treasure! | | |
| 5 | I hope I'm going to be able to go swimming tomorrow. | | |
| 6 | I believe this is what we've been looking for all day. | | |
| 7 | I won't take you to see the lions until you are wearing shoes. | | |
| 8 | Angelina doesn't want to eat pizza for dinner. | | |
| 9 | Michele said she'd bring a dessert to the picnic on Saturday. | | |
| 10 | The dog shouldn't eat candy. | | |

# CONTRACTIONS
## Quiz-Quiz-Trade

**Instructions:** Cut out each card along the dotted line. Then fold each card in half so the question is on one side and the answer is on the back. Glue or tape the cards together to keep the answers and questions on opposite sides.

### 1. Question
Which contraction correctly completes the following sentence?

The students _____ arrive until the bell rings.

a. isn't
b. won't
c. aren't
d. doesn't

### 1. Answer
b. won't

### 2. Question
Which contraction correctly completes the following sentence?

_____ going to make it to lunch.

a. Aren't
b. Isn't
c. He's
d. Doesn't

### 2. Answer
c. He's

### 3. Question
Which contraction correctly completes the following sentence?

Michael _____ going to sing in the school talent show.

a. can't
b. isn't
c. won't
d. shouldn't

### 3. Answer
b. isn't

Cooperative Learning & Grammar
Kagan Publishing • 1 (800) 933-2667 • www.KaganOnline.com

# CONTRACTIONS
## Quiz-Quiz-Trade

**Instructions:** Cut out each card along the dotted line. Then fold each card in half so the question is on one side and the answer is on the back. Glue or tape the cards together to keep the answers and questions on opposite sides.

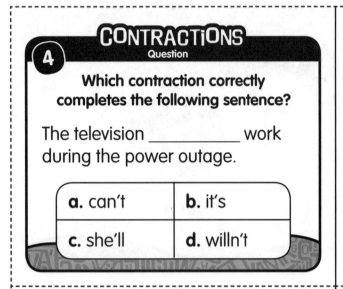
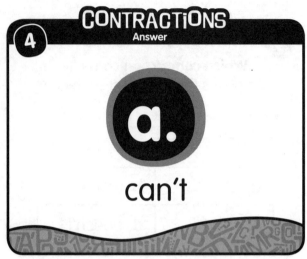
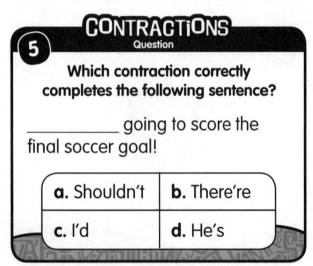

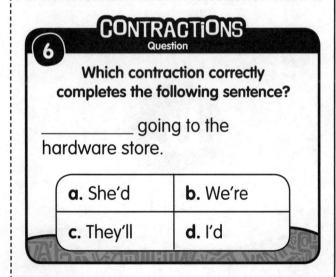

142  Parts of Speech

**Cooperative Learning & Grammar**
Kagan Publishing • 1 (800) 933-2667 • www.KaganOnline.com

**Instructions:** Cut out each card along the dotted line. Then fold each card in half so the question is on one side and the answer is on the back. Glue or tape the cards together to keep the answers and questions on opposite sides.

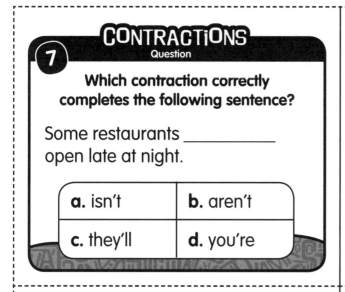

**7** — **CONTRACTIONS** Question

Which contraction correctly completes the following sentence?

Some restaurants _____ open late at night.

- a. isn't
- b. aren't
- c. they'll
- d. you're

**7** — **CONTRACTIONS** Answer

**b.** aren't

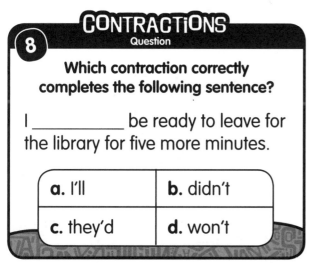

**8** — **CONTRACTIONS** Question

Which contraction correctly completes the following sentence?

I _____ be ready to leave for the library for five more minutes.

- a. I'll
- b. didn't
- c. they'd
- d. won't

**8** — **CONTRACTIONS** Answer

**d.** won't

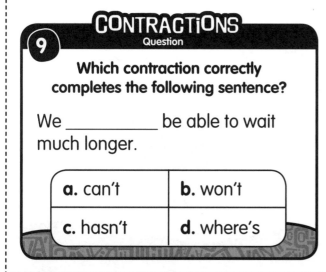

**9** — **CONTRACTIONS** Question

Which contraction correctly completes the following sentence?

We _____ be able to wait much longer.

- a. can't
- b. won't
- c. hasn't
- d. where's

**9** — **CONTRACTIONS** Answer

**b.** won't

**Cooperative Learning & Grammar**
Kagan Publishing • 1 (800) 933-2667 • www.KaganOnline.com

# CONTRACTIONS
## Quiz-Quiz-Trade

**Instructions:** Cut out each card along the dotted line. Then fold each card in half so the question is on one side and the answer is on the back. Glue or tape the cards together to keep the answers and questions on opposite sides.

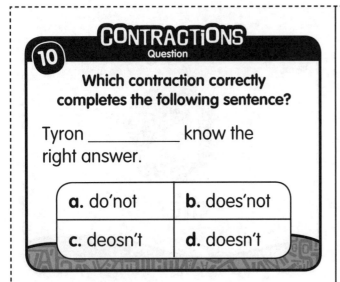

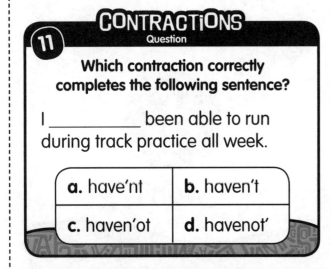

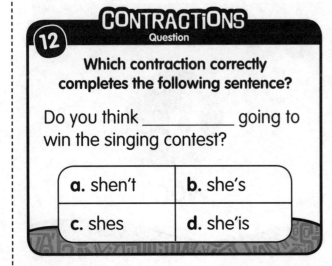

144 Parts of Speech

**Cooperative Learning & Grammar**
Kagan Publishing • 1 (800) 933-2667 • www.KaganOnline.com

**Instructions:** Cut out each card along the dotted line. Then fold each card in half so the question is on one side and the answer is on the back. Glue or tape the cards together to keep the answers and questions on opposite sides.

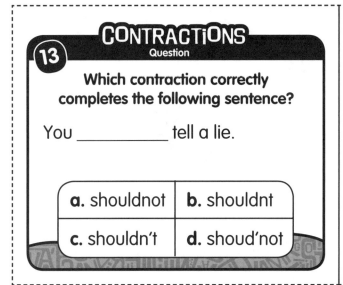

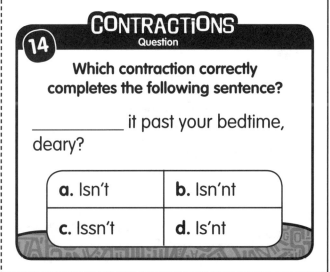

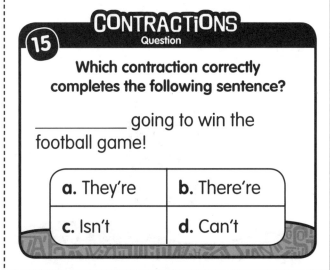

**Instructions:** Cut out each card along the dotted line. Then fold each card in half so the question is on one side and the answer is on the back. Glue or tape the cards together to keep the answers and questions on opposite sides.

### 16 — Question
**CONTRACTIONS**

Which contraction correctly completes the following sentence?

_____ been to the zoo to see the giant turtles.

| a. Won't | b. Shouldn't |
| c. We've | d. We're |

### 16 — Answer
**c. We've**

### 17 — Question
**CONTRACTIONS**

Which contraction correctly completes the following sentence?

I hope _____ be able to go with us.

| a. there're | b. he's |
| c. they'll | d. where's |

### 17 — Answer
**c. they'll**

### 18 — Question
**CONTRACTIONS**

Which contraction correctly completes the following sentence?

_____ not have to find the key if the chest would open.

| a. We'd | b. She's |
| c. They're | d. Hasn't |

### 18 — Answer
**a. We'd**

# CONTRACTIONS
## Quiz-Quiz-Trade

**Instructions:** Cut out each card along the dotted line. Then fold each card in half so the question is on one side and the answer is on the back. Glue or tape the cards together to keep the answers and questions on opposite sides.

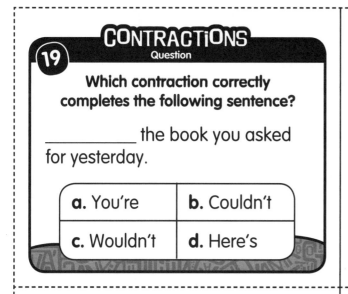

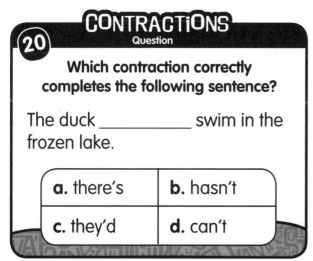

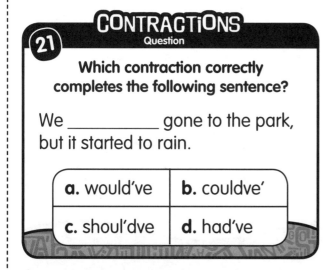

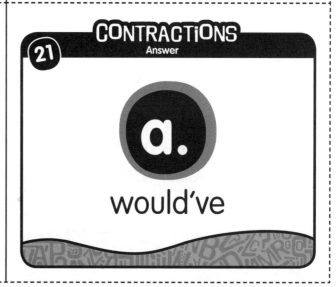

**Cooperative Learning & Grammar**

# CONTRACTIONS
## Quiz-Quiz-Trade

**Instructions:** Cut out each card along the dotted line. Then fold each card in half so the question is on one side and the answer is on the back. Glue or tape the cards together to keep the answers and questions on opposite sides.

**1.** Which 2 words make up the contraction *she's*?

**Answer 1:** she is

**2.** Which 2 words make up the contraction *wouldn't*?

**Answer 2:** would not

**3.** Which 2 words make up the contraction *aren't*?

**Answer 3:** are not

148 Parts of Speech

Cooperative Learning & Grammar
Kagan Publishing • 1 (800) 933-2667 • www.KaganOnline.com

**Instructions:** Cut out each card along the dotted line. Then fold each card in half so the question is on one side and the answer is on the back. Glue or tape the cards together to keep the answers and questions on opposite sides.

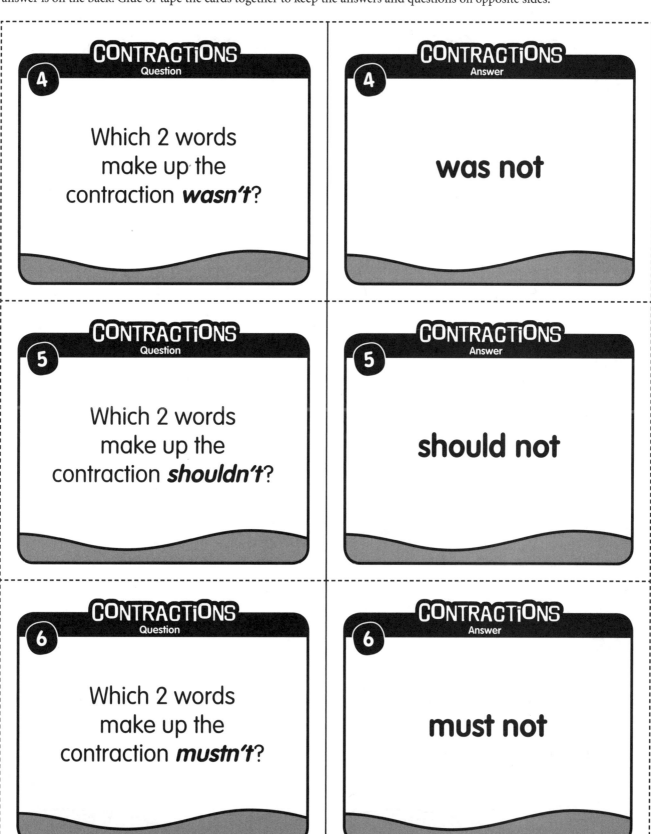

# CONTRACTIONS
## Quiz-Quiz-Trade

**Instructions:** Cut out each card along the dotted line. Then fold each card in half so the question is on one side and the answer is on the back. Glue or tape the cards together to keep the answers and questions on opposite sides.

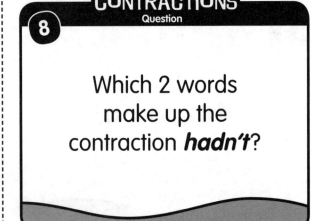

# CONTRACTIONS
## Quiz-Quiz-Trade

**Instructions:** Cut out each card along the dotted line. Then fold each card in half so the question is on one side and the answer is on the back. Glue or tape the cards together to keep the answers and questions on opposite sides.

**CONTRACTIONS — Question 10:** Which 2 words make up the contraction *hasn't*?

**CONTRACTIONS — Answer 10:** has not

**CONTRACTIONS — Question 11:** Which 2 words make up the contraction *didn't*?

**CONTRACTIONS — Answer 11:** did not

**CONTRACTIONS — Question 12:** Which 2 words make up the contraction *haven't*?

**CONTRACTIONS — Answer 12:** have not

**Instructions:** Cut out each card along the dotted line. Then fold each card in half so the question is on one side and the answer is on the back. Glue or tape the cards together to keep the answers and questions on opposite sides.

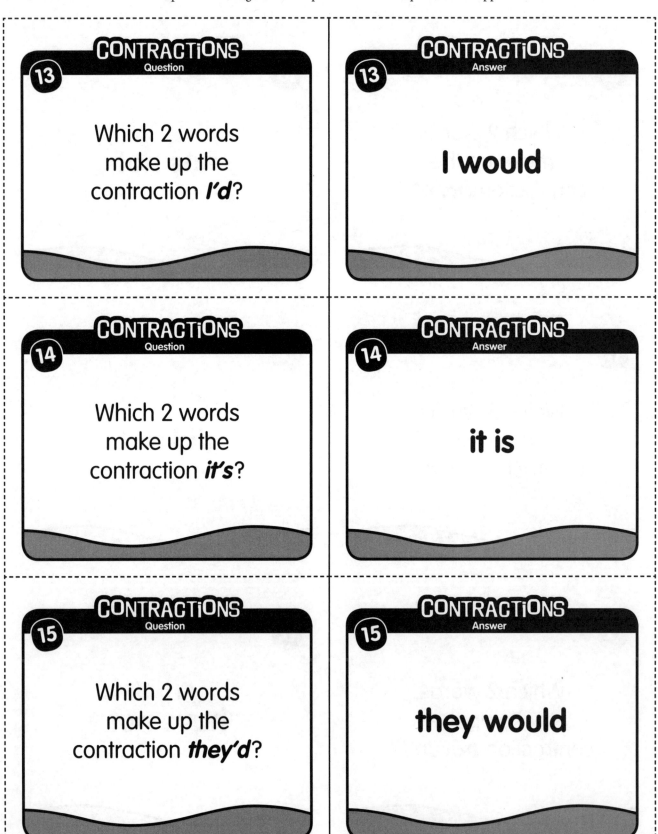

**Instructions:** Cut out each card along the dotted line. Then fold each card in half so the question is on one side and the answer is on the back. Glue or tape the cards together to keep the answers and questions on opposite sides.

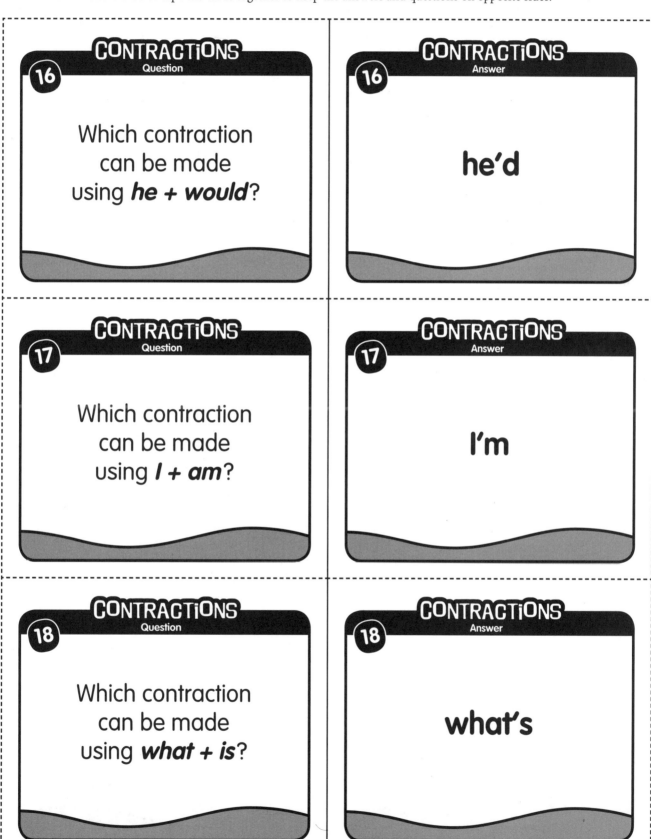

Cooperative Learning & Grammar

**Instructions:** Cut out each card along the dotted line. Then fold each card in half so the question is on one side and the answer is on the back. Glue or tape the cards together to keep the answers and questions on opposite sides.

**CONTRACTIONS** — Question 19: Which contraction can be made using **we + would**?

**CONTRACTIONS** — Answer 19: **we'd**

**CONTRACTIONS** — Question 20: Which 2 words make up the contraction **who's**?

**CONTRACTIONS** — Answer 20: **who is**

**CONTRACTIONS** — Question 21: Which 2 words make up the contraction **we're**?

**CONTRACTIONS** — Answer 21: **we are**

**Instructions:** Cut out each card along the dotted line. Then fold each card in half so the question is on one side and the answer is on the back. Glue or tape the cards together to keep the answers and questions on opposite sides.

**Cooperative Learning & Grammar**

# CONTRACTIONS
## Quiz-Quiz-Trade

**Instructions:** Cut out each card along the dotted line. Then fold each card in half so the question is on one side and the answer is on the back. Glue or tape the cards together to keep the answers and questions on opposite sides.

### 25 — Question
Which contraction can be made using **I + have**?

### 25 — Answer
I've

### 26 — Question
Which contraction can be made using **there + is**?

### 26 — Answer
there's

### 27 — Question
Which contraction can be made using **will + not**?

### 27 — Answer
won't

# Prepositions
## RallyCoach/Sage-N-Scribe

**Instructions:** Circle the preposition(s) in each sentence (if there are any). Take turns working with your partner to solve the problems using RallyCoach or Sage-N-Scribe.

## Partner A

Name _____

1. The box broke open and balls started bouncing down the stairwell.
2. Justin took his math test in green crayon to be funny.
3. Many fruits and berries are edible.
4. Many varieties of grapes are sweet.
5. Other fruits are sour to the taste.
6. Lemons are sour in taste.
7. My cat, Tigger, is hiding under the stairs.
8. Kay waited until the ship disappeared beyond the horizon.
9. Black smoke rose up the chimney.
10. I was searching for my cell phone all morning.

## Partner B

Name _____

1. Grapes and kiwifruit are popular as snacks.
2. Apples are delicious.
3. The vitamins in vegetables are helpful.
4. Most fruits are juicy.
5. The baseball rolled underneath the truck.
6. You can find the office right by the cafeteria.
7. Please be quiet during the movie.
8. The bullet went right through the thick wood.
9. Erica raced into the backyard where the other kids were playing.
10. It has been months since we rented a movie.

## Grammar Skills 3
# PUNCTUATION

- **Capital Letters** (Find-N-Fix) ..................... 160
- **Capital Letters**
  (RallyCoach/Sage-N-Scribe) ................. 161–162
- **Capital Letters** (Find Someone Who) ........... 163
- **Capital Letters**
  (Showdown/Fan-N-Pick) ..................... 164–166
- **Capitalization of Proper Nouns**
  (RallyCoach/Sage-N-Scribe) ..................... 167
- **Capital Letters** (Mix-N-Match) ............. 168–171
- **Commas** (Find-N-Fix) ............................ 172
- **Commas in a Series, Dates & Locations**
  (RallyCoach/Sage-N-Scribe) ................ 173–174
- **Commas** (Find Someone Who) ................. 175
- **Punctuation** (Find-N-Fix) ....................... 176
- **Punctuation** (Find Someone Who) ....... 177–179

- **Punctuation** (Mix-N-Match) ............... 180–183
- **Using Quotation Marks**
  (RallyCoach/Sage-N-Scribe) ..................... 184
- **Quotation Marks & Punctuation**
  (Find Someone Who) ............................. 185
- **Quotation Marks** (Quiz-Quiz-Trade) .... 186–191
- **Capital Letters & Punctuation**
  (RallyCoach/Sage-N-Scribe) ............... 192–193
- **Capital Letters & Punctuation**
  (Find Someone Who) ........................ 194–195
- **Capitalization & Punctuation**
  (Quiz-Quiz-Trade) ............................. 196–203
- **Answer Key** ................................... 247–250

# CAPITAL LETTERS
## Find-N-Fix

Name _____

**Instructions:** For each set of problems, find the incorrect sentence. Indicate which is incorrect using your Find-N-Fix cards. When your team agrees, fix the incorrect problem.

**1** Which sentence does not have capital letters in the correct place?

1. I went to the McDonald's house yesterday.
2. My Dog likes to chase his tail.
3. We will see a movie on Sunday.

**2** Which sentence does not have capital letters in the correct place?

1. sue enjoyed watching the soccer match.
2. Flag Day is celebrated in June.
3. We will be at our grandparents for Christmas.

**3** Which sentence does not have capital letters in the correct place?

1. I used to live in st. louis, missouri.
2. We watched a movie last night on TV.
3. The captain of the ship steered the boat.

**4** Which sentence does not have capital letters in the correct place?

1. Mr. Smith lives on parkdale avenue.
2. He likes to feed the furry squirrels.
3. Don't forget to bring home some milk.

**5** Which sentence does not have capital letters in the correct place?

1. The Chinese restaurant served egg soup.
2. The Swimming pool was 12 feet deep.
3. Louis found a dime on the ground.

160 Punctuation

**Cooperative Learning & Grammar**
Kagan Publishing • 1 (800) 933-2667 • www.KaganOnline.com

# CAPITAL LETTERS
## RallyCoach/Sage-N-Scribe

**Instructions:** Take turns working with your partner to rewrite each sentence using correct capitalization. Use RallyCoach or Sage-N-Scribe to solve the problems.

## Partner A

Name _____

**1.** becky and john traveled to new york with their family for summer vacation.

**2.** aunt shawna and uncle kyle got zoey a teddy bear for her birthday.

**3.** when will we be able to visit the san diego zoo in may?

## Partner B

Name _____

**1.** on monday we will go to dallas, texas, and on wednesday we will travel to houston, texas.

**2.** the vinton family owns the ice cream store.

**3.** danielle lives on booneville street in kansas city, missouri, with her sister mary.

# CAPITAL LETTERS
## RallyCoach/Sage-N-Scribe

**Instructions:** Take turns working with your partner to choose the part of the sentence that needs a capital letter. If there are no errors, choose none. Use RallyCoach or Sage-N-Scribe to solve the problems.

## PARTNER A

Name _____

**1.** Jim and dee went to watch fireworks on the Fourth of July.
- a. Jim and dee
- b. went to watch fireworks
- c. on the Fourth of July.
- d. None

**2.** the car is red with a black stripe down the center.
- a. the car is red
- b. with a black stripe
- c. down the center.
- d. None

**3.** I got to play in the snow in December with my best friend Megan.
- a. I got to play
- b. in the snow in December
- c. with my best friend Megan.
- d. None

**4.** Danny and Jacob went to see the new York yankees play.
- a. Danny and Jacob
- b. went to see
- c. the new York yankees play.
- d. None

## PARTNER B

Name _____

**1.** America celebrates flag day in June.
- a. America celebrates
- b. flag day
- c. in June.
- d. None

**2.** kyle won first place in the track meet on Friday.
- a. kyle won first
- b. place in the track
- c. meet on Friday.
- d. None

**3.** George and his grandfather go to lake pomme de terre to go fishing.
- a. George and his grandfather
- b. go to lake pomme de terre
- c. to go fishing.
- d. None

**4.** Clint rode his bike down Third Street to go to the local market.
- a. Clint rode his bike
- b. down Third Street
- c. to go to the local market.
- d. None

# CAPITAL LETTERS
## Find Someone Who

Name _____

**Instructions:** Pair up and take turns circling the words in each sentence that need a capital letter. Don't forget to get your partner's initials.

**1**
i was born on december 6 in branson, Missouri.

Initials

**2**
my sister will go to chicago in july with mr. williams.

Initials

**3**
michelle and i won't be able to attend the party.

Initials

**4**
superfudge is my favorite book.

Initials

**5**
Do you think molly's burgers or frank's taco stand has the best french fries?

Initials

**6**
my dog rocco jumped in the lake.

Initials

**7**
dear grandma,...

Initials

**8**
bill and tom went to bryant park on wednesday.

Initials

**9**
who has traveled to the atlantic ocean?

Initials

*Cooperative Learning & Grammar*
Kagan Publishing • 1 (800) 933-2667 • www.KaganOnline.com

Punctuation  163

## CAPITAL LETTERS
### Showdown/Fan-N-Pick

**Instructions:** Cut out each card along the dotted line. Give each team a set of cards to play Fan-N-Pick or Showdown.

---

**CAPITAL LETTERS**

**1** Which words in the sentence should be capitalized?

We went to the movies and saw snow white.

---

**CAPITAL LETTERS**

**2** Which word in the sentence should be capitalized?

john walked down the street.

---

**CAPITAL LETTERS**

**3** Which word in the sentence should be capitalized?

My birthday is in july.

---

**CAPITAL LETTERS**

**4** Which word in the sentence should be capitalized?

Tomorrow I am moving to alaska.

---

**CAPITAL LETTERS**

**5** Which word in the sentence should be capitalized?

We will go on our field trip on monday.

---

**CAPITAL LETTERS**

**6** Which word in the sentence should be capitalized?

i live in Branson, Missouri.

# CAPITAL LETTERS
## Showdown/Fan-N-Pick

**Instructions:** Cut out each card along the dotted line. Give each team a set of cards to play Fan-N-Pick or Showdown.

---

**CAPITAL LETTERS**

**7** Which word in the sentence should be capitalized?

My parents shop at minimart.

---

**CAPITAL LETTERS**

**8** Which word in the sentence should be capitalized?

Mr. dawson ate six worms.

---

**CAPITAL LETTERS**

**9** Which word in the sentence should be capitalized?

Dylan and hunter took a walk.

---

**CAPITAL LETTERS**

**10** Which word in the sentence should be capitalized?

who wants to go to the movies?

---

**CAPITAL LETTERS**

**11** Which words in the sentence should be capitalized?

Ms. Kern read *kingdom keepers* to the class.

---

**CAPITAL LETTERS**

**12** Which word in the sentence should be capitalized?

I was born on christmas.

---

*Cooperative Learning & Grammar*
Kagan Publishing • 1 (800) 933-2667 • www.KaganOnline.com

# CAPITAL LETTERS
## Showdown/Fan-N-Pick

**Instructions:** Cut out each card along the dotted line. Give each team a set of cards to play Fan-N-Pick or Showdown.

---

**CAPITAL LETTERS**

**13.** Which part of the sentence does not have the correct capitalization? If no capital letter is needed, select none.

a. Each wednesday
b. my sister has
c. piano practice.
d. None

---

**CAPITAL LETTERS**

**14.** Which part of the sentence does not have the correct capitalization? If no capital letter is needed, select none.

a. My family
b. lives on main street
c. in Chicago.
d. None

---

**CAPITAL LETTERS**

**15.** Which part of the sentence does not have the correct capitalization? If no capital letter is needed, select none.

a. How often
b. does Mark go
c. to Wisconsin?
d. None

---

**CAPITAL LETTERS**

**16.** Which part of the sentence does not have the correct capitalization? If no capital letter is needed, select none.

a. i really
b. enjoy eating at Pizza Palace
c. for dinner.
d. None

---

**CAPITAL LETTERS**

**17.** Which part of the sentence does not have the correct capitalization? If no capital letter is needed, select none.

a. This week
b. my family got a
c. new dog named hunter.
d. None

---

**CAPITAL LETTERS**

**18.** Which part of the sentence does not have the correct capitalization? If no capital letter is needed, select none.

a. Grandma
b. will be visiting
c. this christmas.
d. None

# Capitalization of Proper Nouns
## RallyCoach/Sage-N-Scribe

**Instructions:** Take turns working with your partner to choose the word(s) that needs to be capitalized because it is a proper noun. Use RallyCoach or Sage-N-Scribe to solve the problems.

## Partner A

Name _____

1. 
   a. park
   b. mississippi river
   c. boat
   d. swing

2. 
   a. television
   b. car
   c. street
   d. pizza palace

3. 
   a. branson elementary school
   b. principal
   c. teacher
   d. school assembly

4. 
   a. sports
   b. football
   c. new england patriots
   d. helmet

5. 
   a. mrs. hirarhara
   b. sister
   c. nurse
   d. police officer

## Partner A

Name _____

1. 
   a. flag day
   b. holiday
   c. summer
   d. swimming

2. 
   a. friend
   b. maria
   c. paper
   d. girl

3. 
   a. dentist
   b. bear
   c. ohio
   d. school

4. 
   a. dr. smith
   b. ice cream
   c. circus
   d. ocean

5. 
   a. dog
   b. wednesday
   c. post office
   d. book

*Cooperative Learning & Grammar*
Kagan Publishing • 1 (800) 933-2667 • www.KaganOnline.com

Punctuation 167

# CAPITAL LETTERS Mix-N-Match

**Instructions:** Cut out the cards on the dotted line. Give one card to each student. Distribute cards in sequence so for every student with an Uncapitalized Word card, there is a student with a matching Capitalized Word card.

---

### CAPITAL LETTERS

Which word(s) in the sentence need a capital letter?

My birthday is on saturday.

*Uncapitalized Word*

---

### CAPITAL LETTERS

Why does this word need to be capitalized?

Saturday

*Capitalized Word*

---

### CAPITAL LETTERS

Which word(s) in the sentence need a capital letter?

When will easter be here?

*Uncapitalized Word*

---

### CAPITAL LETTERS

Why does this word need to be capitalized?

Easter

*Capitalized Word*

---

### CAPITAL LETTERS

Which word(s) in the sentence need a capital letter?

i don't enjoy broccoli.

*Uncapitalized Word*

---

### CAPITAL LETTERS

Why does this word need to be capitalized?

I

*Capitalized Word*

*Cooperative Learning & Grammar*
Kagan Publishing • 1 (800) 933-2667 • www.KaganOnline.com

# CAPITAL LETTERS Mix-N-Match

**Instructions:** Cut out the cards on the dotted line. Give one card to each student. Distribute cards in sequence so for every student with an Uncapitalized Word card, there is a student with a matching Capitalized Word card.

---

**CAPITAL LETTERS**

Which word(s) in the sentence need a capital letter?

Brent and sue went to the park.

*Uncapitalized Word*

---

**CAPITAL LETTERS**

Why does this word need to be capitalized?

Sue

*Capitalized Word*

---

**CAPITAL LETTERS**

Which word(s) in the sentence need a capital letter?

My favorite book is *charlotte's web.*

*Uncapitalized Word*

---

**CAPITAL LETTERS**

Why do these words need to be capitalized?

*Charlotte's Web*

*Capitalized Word*

---

**CAPITAL LETTERS**

Which word(s) in the sentence need a capital letter?

What time is the party at birthday world?

*Uncapitalized Word*

---

**CAPITAL LETTERS**

Why do these words need to be capitalized?

Birthday World

*Capitalized Word*

# CAPITAL LETTERS
## Mix-N-Match

**Instructions:** Cut out the cards on the dotted line. Give one card to each student. Distribute cards in sequence so for every student with an Uncapitalized Word card, there is a student with a matching Capitalized Word card.

---

**CAPITAL LETTERS**

Which word(s) in the sentence need a capital letter?

We live in branson.

*Uncapitalized Word*

---

**CAPITAL LETTERS**

Why does this word need to be capitalized?

Branson

*Capitalized Word*

---

**CAPITAL LETTERS**

Which word(s) in the sentence need a capital letter?

mr. Brown will be our substitute.

*Uncapitalized Word*

---

**CAPITAL LETTERS**

Why does this word need to be capitalized?

Mr.

*Capitalized Word*

---

**CAPITAL LETTERS**

Which word(s) in the sentence need a capital letter?

arkansas is a nice place to live.

*Uncapitalized Word*

---

**CAPITAL LETTERS**

Why does this word need to be capitalized?

Arkansas

*Capitalized Word*

---

170 Punctuation

Cooperative Learning & Grammar
Kagan Publishing • 1 (800) 933-2667 • www.KaganOnline.com

# CAPITAL LETTERS
## Mix-N-Match

**Instructions:** Cut out the cards on the dotted line. Give one card to each student. Distribute cards in sequence so for every student with an Uncapitalized Word card, there is a student with a matching Capitalized Word card.

---

**CAPITAL LETTERS**

Which word(s) in the sentence need a capital letter?

Which month comes after september?

*Uncapitalized Word*

---

**CAPITAL LETTERS**

Why does this word need to be capitalized?

September

*Capitalized Word*

---

**CAPITAL LETTERS**

Which word(s) in the sentence need a capital letter?

My dog jake fetches balls.

*Uncapitalized Word*

---

**CAPITAL LETTERS**

Why does this word need to be capitalized?

Jake

*Capitalized Word*

---

**CAPITAL LETTERS**

Which word(s) in the sentence need a capital letter?

Mr. Smith teaches at mark twain elementary.

*Uncapitalized Word*

---

**CAPITAL LETTERS**

Why do these words need to be capitalized?

Mark Twain Elementary

*Capitalized Word*

# COMMAS
## Find-N-Fix

Name _____

**Instructions:** For each set of problems, find the incorrect sentence. Indicate which is incorrect using your Find-N-Fix cards. When your team agrees, fix the incorrect problem.

**1. Which sentence does not have commas in the correct place?**
1. My father was born in Branson, Missouri.
2. This summer we will be visiting Florida Alabama and Kentucky.
3. My dog Rocco likes to fetch newspapers, sticks, and balls.

**2. Which sentence does not have commas in the correct place?**
1. My sister's birthday is on October 4, 1998.
2. This weekend we went to grandma's house, watched a movie, and went swimming.
3. On July 4 1776 we claimed our independence from the British.

**3. Which sentence does not have commas in the correct place?**
1. I went to the park with Stacey Erin, and Sue.
2. Mrs. Smith has a comb, lipstick, and mirror in her purse.
3. Mike has a carrot, sandwich, and pudding in his lunch.

**4. Which sentence does not have commas in the correct place?**
1. Joe will swim, ride, and hike at camp.
2. Robins can fly sing, and build nests.
3. Lori got a bracelet, book, and hamster for her birthday.

**5. Which sentence does not have commas in the correct place?**
1. It rained all day Monday, Tuesday, and Wednesday.
2. Mom fixed peas corn and tomatoes for dinner last night.
3. We ate turkey, pie, and mashed potatoes at Thanksgiving dinner.

172 Punctuation

**Cooperative Learning & Grammar**
Kagan Publishing • 1 (800) 933-2667 • www.KaganOnline.com

# Commas in a Series, Dates & Locations
## RallyCoach/Sage-N-Scribe

**Instructions:** Take turns working with your partner to correctly add commas to each sentence. Use RallyCoach or Sage-N-Scribe to solve the problems.

### Partner A

Name _____

1. Jason wanted to take a ball blanket and umbrella to the beach.

2. Becky was born on December 3 1998.

3. Megan Sara Jade and Cassidy wanted to play on the slide during recess.

4. This summer my family is taking a vacation to Baltimore Maryland.

5. I live at 453 Elm Street in Cleveland Ohio.

6. On June 28 2012 we will be going to Orlando Florida to visit my grandparents.

7. It rained all day on Wednesday Thursday and Friday.

8. My favorite colors are purple blue yellow and white.

9. School started on August 27 2010.

10. Mrs. Mazen read us a story about a bat an old woman and a shoe.

### Partner B

Name _____

1. Mom gave me a peanut butter sandwich apple and juice for my lunch.

2. Mr. Burns was born on September 17 1983.

3. I have six cats three dogs and ten goldfish for pets.

4. Bobby went to the store and bought soda cookies crackers and candy for his campout.

5. Uncle Rusty moved to Mason Mississippi for his new job.

6. I got a new bicycle a bouncy ball and a harmonica for my birthday.

7. Our cat had her kittens on July 9 2007.

8. We didn't have school Monday Tuesday or Wednesday because of the snow.

9. I needed to pack my toothbrush washcloth and shampoo for my trip to grandmother's.

10. Papa and Nana were married June 27 1970.

# Commas in a Series, Dates & Locations
## RallyCoach/Sage-N-Scribe

**Instructions:** Take turns working with your partner to choose the sentence that uses commas correctly. Use RallyCoach or Sage-N-Scribe to solve the problems.

## Partner A

Name _____

**1.**
a. Kolby's birthday was July 16, 2008.
b. Kolby's birthday, was July 16 2008.
c. Kolby's birthday was, July 16 2008.

**2.**
a. My family visits Branson, Missouri, every year.
b. My family visits Branson Missouri every year.
c. My family visits, Branson, Missouri every year.

**3.**
a. We need to get eggs milk and bread at the market.
b. We need to get, eggs, milk, and bread at the market.
c. We need to get eggs, milk, and bread at the market.

**4.**
a. Our plane flew from Denver, Colorado to Atlanta Georgia.
b. Our plane flew from Denver, Colorado, to Atlanta, Georgia.
c. Our plane flew from Denver, Colorado to Atlanta Georgia.

## Partner B

Name _____

**1.**
a. My parents' anniversary was December, 26 1982.
b. My parents' anniversary was December 26, 1982.
c. My parents' anniversary was December, 26, 1982.

**2.**
a. My favorite colors are purple, pink, and red.
b. My favorite colors are, purple, pink, and, red.
c. My favorite colors are purple pink and red.

**3.**
a. I was born in New York New, York.
b. I was born in New, York, New, York,
c. I was born in New York, New York.

**4.**
a. We will visit my grandma on June 3, 2012 in Orlando Florida.
b. We will visit my grandma on June 3 2012 in Orlando Florida.
c. We will visit my grandma on June 3, 2012, in Orlando, Florida.

**Name** _____

**Instructions:** Pair up and take turns putting commas in the correct places in the sentences below. Don't forget to get your partner's initials.

1. The four largest countries in the world are Russia Canada China and the United States.

2. The Pilgrims came to Plymouth Rock Massachusetts.

3. Baseball soccer and football are popular high school sports.

4. Washington Lincoln Kennedy and Truman were important presidents.

5. Mercury Venus Earth and Mars are the planets closest to the sun.

6. The Constitution of the United States was adopted on September 17 1787.

7. President Abraham Lincoln was assassinated on April 14 1865.

8. The Empire State building is located in New York City New York.

9. The Pacific Arctic Indian and Atlantic Oceans make up most of the earth's water.

10. My grandma planted lettuce tomatoes spinach and squash in her summer garden.

# Punctuation
## Find-N-Fix

Name _____

**Instructions:** For each set of problems, find the incorrect sentence. Indicate which is incorrect using your Find-N-Fix cards. When your team agrees, fix the incorrect problem.

**1. Which sentence does not have the correct punctuation?**
1. Sally and I went to the store.
2. What time is it.
3. Jason took a walk through the park.

**2. Which sentence does not have the correct punctuation?**
1. Football is my favorite sport?
2. What is your favorite sport?
3. Where is your lunch box?

**3. Which sentence does not have the correct punctuation?**
1. What time is school out?
2. Wow that is amazing!
3. Do you know where the library is.

**4. Which sentence does not have the correct punctuation?**
1. I went on vacation to Florida?
2. Would you care for an apple?
3. How do you spell *cat*?

**5. Which sentence does not have the correct punctuation?**
1. The sun is too bright!
2. My dog is black and brown.
3. Where is the waterfall.

# Punctuation
## Find Someone Who

Name _____

**Instructions:** Pair up and take turns putting the correct punctuation at the end of each sentence. Don't forget to get your partner's initials.

**1.** Who do you think will win on the game show ___

Initials

**2.** My birthday is in December ___

Initials

**3.** Watch out ___

Initials

**4.** I had a peanut butter sandwich for lunch ___

Initials

**5.** What time does the movie start ___

Initials

**6.** When will mom bring the cookies to school ___

Initials

**7.** Oh no ___

Initials

**8.** Get out your pens and pencils for writing ___

Initials

**9.** Did you have a good weekend ___

Initials

# Punctuation
## Find Someone Who

Name _____

**Instructions:** Pair up and take turns determining the correct punctuation for the end of each sentence. Circle the correct answer. Don't forget to get your partner's initials.

**1** When will we be there
- a. .
- b. ?
- c. !

Initials _____

**2** What a cute puppy
- a. .
- b. ?
- c. !

Initials _____

**3** I love to play football
- a. .
- b. ?
- c. !

Initials _____

**4** The dog is black
- a. .
- b. ?
- c. !

Initials _____

**5** What time is lunch
- a. .
- b. ?
- c. !

Initials _____

**6** Oh, thank you for the present
- a. .
- b. ?
- c. !

Initials _____

**7** Have you seen my missing sock
- a. .
- b. ?
- c. !

Initials _____

**8** My favorite color is purple
- a. .
- b. ?
- c. !

Initials _____

**9** I want to go swimming
- a. .
- b. ?
- c. !

Initials _____

**Punctuation — Find Someone Who**

Name _____

**Instructions:** Pair up and take turns choosing the sentence with correct punctuation. Don't forget to get your partner's initials.

### 1
- **a.** Marlene wants to go to the zoo for her birthday?
- **b.** May I go use the restroom.
- **c.** Maggie is learning to climb the stairs all by herself.
- **d.** On Friday, I am going to the amusement park?

Initials

### 2
- **a.** When will we be going to the library?
- **b.** My favorite show on television is about horses and dogs?
- **c.** I am eating macaroni and cheese for dinner!
- **d.** What is your favorite color.

Initials

### 3
- **a.** I have a pencil backpack and a notebook for my first day at school.
- **b.** "Mommy, can I have a cheeseburger?" asked Fred.
- **c.** Minnie needs to pick up her toys?
- **d.** I want to go to the tree to see the birds nest?

Initials

### 4
- **a.** Happy birthday Natalie?
- **b.** At the market we bought apples, bananas, and oranges for our picnic.
- **c.** When can we go to the park!
- **d.** "I have to do my math homework!"

Initials

### 5
- **a.** The firefighters made a presentation at our school yesterday?
- **b.** I helped my mom do the laundry.
- **c.** I like to play on the slides swings and monkey bars at recess.
- **d.** My birthday was last month!

Initials

### 6
- **a.** That roller coaster was so much fun!
- **b.** Why did that puppy dog growl at the cat.
- **c.** Jenny wants to go to the movies tomorrow?
- **d.** My favorite snack to eat is popcorn?

Initials

*Cooperative Learning & Grammar*
Kagan Publishing • 1 (800) 933-2667 • www.KaganOnline.com

**Instructions:** Cut out the cards on the dotted line. Give one card to each student. Distribute cards in sequence so for every student with a Sentence card, there is a student with a matching Punctuation Mark card.

---

**Punctuation — Sentence**

Which punctuation mark completes the sentence?

The ice cream was wonderful

---

**Punctuation — Punctuation Mark**

What type of sentence ends with this mark?

●

---

**Punctuation — Sentence**

Which punctuation mark completes the sentence?

What time does school start

---

**Punctuation — Punctuation Mark**

What type of sentence ends with this mark?

?

---

**Punctuation — Sentence**

Which punctuation mark completes the sentence?

Wow

---

**Punctuation — Punctuation Mark**

What type of sentence ends with this mark?

!

---

180 Punctuation

*Cooperative Learning & Grammar*
Kagan Publishing • 1 (800) 933-2667 • www.KaganOnline.com

**Instructions:** Cut out the cards on the dotted line. Give one card to each student. Distribute cards in sequence so for every student with a Sentence card, there is a student with a matching Punctuation Mark card.

---

**Punctuation — Sentence**

Which punctuation mark completes the sentence?

The clowns were my favorite part of the circus

---

**Punctuation — Punctuation Mark**

What type of sentence ends with this mark?

●

---

**Punctuation — Sentence**

Which punctuation mark completes the sentence?

Did you happen to find my lost mitten

---

**Punctuation — Punctuation Mark**

What type of sentence ends with this mark?

?

---

**Punctuation — Sentence**

Which punctuation mark completes the sentence?

Get out your pencils

---

**Punctuation — Punctuation Mark**

What type of sentence ends with this mark?

●

---

*Cooperative Learning & Grammar*
Kagan Publishing • 1 (800) 933-2667 • www.KaganOnline.com

# Punctuation Mix-N-Match

**Instructions:** Cut out the cards on the dotted line. Give one card to each student. Distribute cards in sequence so for every student with a Sentence card, there is a student with a matching Punctuation Mark card.

---

**PUNCTUATION — Sentence**

Which punctuation mark completes the sentence?

Watch out

---

**PUNCTUATION — Punctuation Mark**

What type of sentence ends with this mark?

!

---

**PUNCTUATION — Sentence**

Which punctuation mark completes the sentence?

Was the supermarket busy

---

**PUNCTUATION — Punctuation Mark**

What type of sentence ends with this mark?

?

---

**PUNCTUATION — Sentence**

Which punctuation mark completes the sentence?

Dana's birthday is on Sunday

---

**PUNCTUATION — Punctuation Mark**

What type of sentence ends with this mark?

.

# Punctuation Mix-N-Match

**Instructions:** Cut out the cards on the dotted line. Give one card to each student. Distribute cards in sequence so for every student with a Sentence card, there is a student with a matching Punctuation Mark card.

---

**Punctuation — Sentence**

Which punctuation mark completes the sentence?

Are you going to look for my camera

---

**Punctuation — Punctuation Mark**

What type of sentence ends with this mark?

?

---

**Punctuation — Sentence**

Which punctuation mark completes the sentence?

Susie plays the piano

---

**Punctuation — Punctuation Mark**

What type of sentence ends with this mark?

.

---

**Punctuation — Sentence**

Which punctuation mark completes the sentence?

Oh my goodness

---

**Punctuation — Punctuation Mark**

What type of sentence ends with this mark?

!

# Using Quotation Marks
## RallyCoach/Sage-N-Scribe

**Instructions:** In the sentences below place quotation marks where needed. Take turns working with your partner to using RallyCoach or Sage-N-Scribe to solve the problems.

### Partner A

Name _____

1. Turn off the lights, Mother said.
2. Mrs. Gordon asked, Daniel, are you going with me?
3. Jennifer replied, I'd love to come to your party.
4. Anna gave a report called, Indians of the Northwest.
5. Are you going to the movies? Millie asked.
6. The teacher said, Maggie, you got 100% on your test.
7. José said, Derek, let's play after school.
8. Luke replied, It's very cold today.
9. Jessica's short story was titled, Five Artists.
10. Denzel asked, Is that a good restaurant?

### Partner B

Name _____

1. Francesca, I'll be home late, said mother.
2. Father said, I'm going to work.
3. Shimah remarked, I have finished my homework.
4. Li asked, How old are you?
5. Let's get together next week, said Dina.
6. Have you read *Charlotte's Web*? asked our teacher.
7. Vinnie asked, Where's the car's light?
8. Aunt Molly said, I'll be home late tonight.
9. How much is the toy car? asked Andrew.
10. Have you read this poem?

# Quotation Marks & Punctuation
## Find Someone Who

Name _____

**Instructions:** Pair up and take turns adding the correct punctuation for each sentence. Don't forget your partner's initials.

**Initials**

1. Ed said let's go to the movies after our club meeting

2. When do you want to finish your homework asked mom

3. I can't wait to go to summer camp said susan because I will be able to ride a horse

4. Megan wondered I hope to be able to visit my grandmother again

5. Mrs. Ipock asked me to take care of the class pet Jared told his dad

6. May I please watch a cartoon Chandler asked his older sister

7. I hope we will be able to see a shooting star declared Emma

8. I love it when my bare feet feels the cool grass squealed Lily to her mom.

9. May I talk with Mr. Barrnet asked the lady on the phone

10. Why do butterflies migrate in the winter asked a student

*Cooperative Learning & Grammar*
Kagan Publishing • 1 (800) 933-2667 • www.KaganOnline.com

# Quotation Marks
## Quiz-Quiz-Trade

**Instructions:** Cut out each card along the dotted line. Then fold each card in half so the question is on one side and the answer is on the back. Glue or tape the cards together to keep the answers and questions on opposite sides.

---

### Quotation Marks

**1.** Which sentence, if needed, correctly uses quotation marks?

a. Jimmy said let's go to the lake.

b. Jimmy said, "Let's go to the lake."

c. "Jimmy said, let's got o the lake."

d. Jimmy" said, let's go to the lake.

---

### Quotation Marks

**1.** b.

Jimmy said, "Let's go to the lake."

---

### Quotation Marks

**2.** Which sentence, if needed, correctly uses quotation marks?

a. Can we go to the movies?" mom asked.

b. "Can we go to the movies? Mom asked."

c. "Can we go to the movies"? mom asked.

d. "Can we go to the movies?" mom asked.

---

### Quotation Marks

**2.** d.

"Can we go the movies?" mom asked.

---

### Quotation Marks

**3.** Which sentence, if needed, correctly uses quotation marks?

a. "Let's have a tea party tomorrow," said Sue.

b. Let's have a tea party tomorrow said Sue.

c. "Let's have a tea party tomorrow said Sue."

d. Let's have a tea party tomorrow." said Sue.

---

### Quotation Marks

**3.** a.

"Let's have a tea party tomorrow," said Sue.

# Quotation Marks
## Quiz-Quiz-Trade

**Instructions:** Cut out each card along the dotted line. Then fold each card in half so the question is on one side and the answer is on the back. Glue or tape the cards together to keep the answers and questions on opposite sides.

---

**QUOTATION MARKS**

**4** Which sentence, if needed, correctly uses quotation marks?

a. I want to see the monkeys shouted! the boy excitedly.

b. I want to see the monkeys! "shouted the boy excitedly."

c. "I want to see the monkeys!" shouted the boy excitedly.

d. "I want to see the monkeys" shouted the boy excitedly!

---

**QUOTATION MARKS**

**4**

**c.**

"I want to see the monkeys!" shouted the boy excitedly.

---

**QUOTATION MARKS**

**5** Which sentence, if needed, correctly uses quotation marks?

a. Peter said, "This concert is the best I have ever seen"!

b. "Peter said, This concert is the best I have ever seen!"

c. Peter said, "This concert is the best I have ever seen!"

d. Peter said, This concert is the best I have ever seen!

---

**QUOTATION MARKS**

**5**

**c.**

Peter said, "This concert is the best I have ever seen!"

---

**QUOTATION MARKS**

**6** Which sentence, if needed, correctly uses quotation marks?

a. "Ouch that hurts Jeffery told the nurse."

b. "Ouch that hurts," Jeffery told the nurse.

c. Ouch that hurts Jeffery told the nurse.

d. "Ouch that hurts," Jeffery told, "the nurse."

---

**QUOTATION MARKS**

**6**

**b.**

"Ouch that hurts," Jeffery told the nurse.

---

*Cooperative Learning & Grammar*
Kagan Publishing • 1 (800) 933-2667 • www.KaganOnline.com

# Quotation Marks
*Quiz-Quiz-Trade*

**Instructions:** Cut out each card along the dotted line. Then fold each card in half so the question is on one side and the answer is on the back. Glue or tape the cards together to keep the answers and questions on opposite sides.

## Quotation Marks

**7.** Which sentence, if needed, correctly uses quotation marks?

a. Jenny wished for a new puppy.

b. Jenny wished, "for a new puppy."

c. Jenny "wished for a new puppy."

d. "Jenny wished for a new puppy".

## Quotation Marks

**7.** a.

Jenny wished for a new puppy.

## Quotation Marks

**8.** Which sentence, if needed, correctly uses quotation marks?

a. The happy couple asked the waiter, "What are tonight's specials"?

b. The happy couple asked the waiter what are tonight's specials.

c. The happy couple asked, "The waiter what are tonight's specials?"

d. The happy couple asked the waiter, "What are tonight's specials?"

## Quotation Marks

**8.** d.

The happy couple asked the waiter, "What are tonight's specials?"

## Quotation Marks

**9.** Which sentence, if needed, correctly uses quotation marks?

a. I am hungry snapped the alligator.

b. "I am hungry," snapped the alligator.

c. I am hungry "snapped the alligator."

d. "I am hungry snapped the alligator."

## Quotation Marks

**9.** b.

"I am hungry," snapped the alligator.

# Quotation Marks
## Quiz-Quiz-Trade

**Instructions:** Cut out each card along the dotted line. Then fold each card in half so the question is on one side and the answer is on the back. Glue or tape the cards together to keep the answers and questions on opposite sides.

---

### QUOTATION MARKS — 10

Which sentence, if needed, correctly uses quotation marks?

a. Megan told me, "Not to go past the corner."
b. "Megan told me not to go past the corner."
c. Megan told me not to go past the corner.
d. Megan told me, not to go past the corner."

**Answer: c.** Megan told me not to go past the corner.

---

### QUOTATION MARKS — 11

Which sentence, if needed, correctly uses quotation marks?

a. "I will have the refrigerator ready by Tuesday, the man said.
b. I will have the refrigerator ready by Tuesday the man said.
c. I will have the refrigerator ready, "By Tuesday the man said."
d. "I will have the refrigerator ready by Tuesday," the man said.

**Answer: d.** "I will have the refrigerator ready by Tuesday," the man said.

---

### QUOTATION MARKS — 12

Which sentence, if needed, correctly uses quotation marks?

a. I hope lunch is ready soon whined Judy because I am hungry.
b. "I hope lunch is ready soon," whined Judy because I am hungry.
c. "I hope lunch is ready soon," whined Judy, "because I am hungry."
d. "I hope lunch is ready soon whined Judy because I am hungry."

**Answer: c.** "I hope lunch is ready soon," whined Judy, "because I am hungry."

---

Cooperative Learning & Grammar
Kagan Publishing • 1 (800) 933-2667 • www.KaganOnline.com

**Instructions:** Cut out each card along the dotted line. Then fold each card in half so the question is on one side and the answer is on the back. Glue or tape the cards together to keep the answers and questions on opposite sides.

## QUOTATION MARKS

**13.** Which sentence, if needed, correctly uses quotation marks?

a. My son sings songs about animals.

b. My son sings, "Songs about animals."

c. My son "Sings songs about animals."

d. "My son sings songs about animals."

## QUOTATION MARKS

**13.**

**a.**

My son sings songs about animals.

## QUOTATION MARKS

**14.** Which sentence, if needed, correctly uses quotation marks?

a. This is so much fun exclaimed Kolby as he got off the roller coaster.

b. "This is so much fun," exclaimed Kolby, "as he got off the roller coaster."

c. This is so much fun exclaimed Kolby. "as he got off the roller coaster."

d. "This is so much fun," exclaimed Kolby as he got off the roller coaster.

## QUOTATION MARKS

**14.**

**d.**

"This is so much fun," exclaimed Kolby as he got off the roller coaster.

## QUOTATION MARKS

**15.** Which sentence, if needed, correctly uses quotation marks?

a. "My favorite flavor of ice cream is strawberry chocolate chip."

b. My favorite flavor of ice cream is strawberry chocolate chip.

c. "My favorite flavor of ice cream" is strawberry chocolate chip.

d. My favorite flavor of ice cream is strawberry chocolate chip."

## QUOTATION MARKS

**15.**

**b.**

My favorite flavor of ice cream is strawberry chocolate chip.

# QUOTATION MARKS
## Quiz-Quiz-Trade

**Instructions:** Cut out each card along the dotted line. Then fold each card in half so the question is on one side and the answer is on the back. Glue or tape the cards together to keep the answers and questions on opposite sides.

---

### QUOTATION MARKS

**16.** Which sentence, if needed, correctly uses quotation marks?

a. "The doctor told me," recalled Jami, "to ice my foot once a day."

b. The doctor told me recalled Jami, "to ice my foot once a day."

c. "The doctor told me recalled Jami to ice my foot once a day."

d. The doctor told me recalled Jami to ice my foot once a day.

---

### QUOTATION MARKS

**16.**

"The doctor told me," recalled Jami, "to ice my foot once a day."

---

### QUOTATION MARKS

**17.** Which sentence, if needed, correctly uses quotation marks?

a. "And the home of the brave sang Sally."

b. And the home of the brave sang Sally.

c. "And the home of the brave," sang Sally.

d. And the home of the brave, "sang Sally.

---

### QUOTATION MARKS

**17.**

"And the home of the brave," sang Sally.

---

### QUOTATION MARKS

**18.** Which sentence, if needed, correctly uses quotation marks?

a. The poster said to be ready by 6 am.

b. The poster said, to be ready by 6 am."

c. "The poster said to be ready by 6 am."

d. The poster said to be ready by 6 am."

---

### QUOTATION MARKS

**18.**

The poster said to be ready by 6 am.

# Capital Letters & Punctuation
## RallyCoach/Sage-N-Scribe

**Instructions:** Take turns working with your partner to rewrite each sentence using correct capitalization and punctuation. Use RallyCoach or Sage-N-Scribe to solve the problems.

## Partner A

Name _____

1. my friend, susan, lives in baltimore maryland

2. molly and maggie like to eat cholcolate ice cream at central park

3. kevin wants to go to orlando florida to swim fish and play at the beach

## Partner B

Name _____

1. patty likes to read mysteries fairy tales and fantasy books

2. when will i be able to return my book to boone county library

3. ellen went to the super eight movie theater to watch her favorite film

# Capital Letters & Punctuation
## RallyCoach/Sage-N-Scribe

**Instructions:** Take turns working with your partner to choose the sentence that has the correct capitalization and punctuation. With your partner solve the problems using RallyCoach or Sage-N-Scribe.

## Partner A

Name _____

**1.**
a. Tomorrow we are going to the san diego zoo.
b. Tomorrow we are going to the San Diego zoo.
c. Tomorrow we are going to the San Diego Zoo.

**2.**
a. I am going to invite Becky Megan and Jenny to my birthday party?
b. I am going to invite Becky, Megan, and Jenny to my birthday party.
c. I am going to invite Becky, Megan, and Jenny to my birthday party

**3.**
a. please pick up your toys before going outside.
b. Please, pick up your toys before going outside
c. Please pick up your toys before going outside.

**4.**
a. My family is visiting london england March, 13.
b. My family is visiting London, England, on March 13.
c. My family is visiting London England March 13.

## Partner B

Name _____

**1.**
a. Our school band is going to perform at The Greene County Fair?
b. Our school band is going to perform at the greene county fair.
c. Our school band is going to perform at the Greene County Fair.

**2.**
a. I am going to a swimming party on June 5, 2011.
b. I am going to a swimming party on June, 5, 2011
c. I am going to a swimming party on June 5, 2011

**3.**
a. I play football, soccer baseball, and golf during the year.
b. I play football, soccer, Baseball, and golf during the year
c. I play football, soccer, baseball, and golf during the year.

**4.**
a. My sister's dance recital is on Sunday at Central High School.
b. My Sister's dance recital is on Sunday at central high school.
c. My sister's dance recital is on sunday at Central, High, School.

*Cooperative Learning & Grammar*

# Capital Letters & Punctuation
## Find Someone Who

Name _____

**Instructions:** Pair up and take turns filling in the circle of each sentence that uses the correct capitalization and punctuation. Don't forget to get your partner's initials.

**1**
- ○ Where is the dog?
- ○ My shirt is blue?
- ○ the bell rang for lunch.

Initials

**2**
- ○ johnny watched a movie last night.
- ○ What time is it in france?
- ○ The pencil is not sharp.

Initials

**3**
- ○ Bailey said she would come over on saturday.
- ○ My mom is making pizza for dinner.
- ○ Tammy and billy are playing ball.

Initials

**4**
- ○ The computer is broken?
- ○ Stop that runaway cart!
- ○ my homework is due tomorrow

Initials

**5**
- ○ My dog loves to chew on its bone.
- ○ What time is dinner
- ○ how do you dial a phone?

Initials

**6**
- ○ The soccer team won its first game
- ○ Jenny likes her friend hanna.
- ○ The pizza was yummy!

Initials

**7**
- ○ My mom is going on vacation
- ○ Florida is really nice in the summer.
- ○ We celebrate flag day in june.

Initials

**8**
- ○ The flower is purple.
- ○ When do we leave for lunch.
- ○ the library is closed

Initials

**9**
- ○ mrs. dewey loves to read
- ○ Which way do I go to the store?
- ○ *because winn-dixie* is my favorite book

Initials

**10**
- ○ Will you help me with this problem?
- ○ a baby kangaroo is called a joey.
- ○ The tennis ball flew over the net

Initials

**11**
- ○ The monkey is looking for its food?
- ○ the snowman melted in the sun.
- ○ The baby is so cute!

Initials

**12**
- ○ the lion escaped from the san diego zoo.
- ○ When will it be warm outside?
- ○ The watch is broken

Initials

# Capital Letters & Punctuation
## Find Someone Who

Name _____

**Instructions:** Pair up and take turns filling in the circle of each sentence that uses the correct capitalization and punctuation. Don't forget to get your partner's initials.

**1**
- ○ the puppy is lost.
- ○ The book, *Charlotte's Web*, is about a spider.
- ○ Where is the gym

Initials

**2**
- ○ The sun is yellow?
- ○ The Picture Fell off the wall.
- ○ It rains a lot in March.

Initials

**3**
- ○ It can get very cold in winter.
- ○ The phone rang all night long
- ○ maybe we can sell comic books

Initials

**4**
- ○ We will go to the market after school
- ○ Dr. Seuss was a great children's author.
- ○ Maybe you can stay at my house on Friday

Initials

**5**
- ○ My brother is playing baseball this Summer.
- ○ What did you do for Christmas?
- ○ this house is dirty!

Initials

**6**
- ○ I broke the lamp
- ○ i hope you are going to finish your chores.
- ○ We are going to the beach this summer.

Initials

**7**
- ○ My favorite animal is a dolphin.
- ○ My family always goes to colorado in the summer.
- ○ When do you want to leave

Initials

**8**
- ○ It snowed three inches yesterday?
- ○ I like your new jeans
- ○ What will happen if I mix green and yellow paint?

Initials

**9**
- ○ How long did you study your spelling words
- ○ Tomorrow i will bring my dog to show and tell.
- ○ My sister went to see Dr. Richmond because she was ill.

Initials

**Cooperative Learning & Grammar**
Kagan Publishing • 1 (800) 933-2667 • www.KaganOnline.com

Punctuation  **195**

# Capitalization & Punctuation
## Quiz-Quiz-Trade

**Instructions:** Cut out each card along the dotted line. Then fold each card in half so the question is on one side and the answer is on the back. Glue or tape the cards together to keep the answers and questions on opposite sides.

### Capitalization & Punctuation — Question 1
Which sentence has correct capitalization and/or punctuation?

a. Don walked his Dog everyday.

b. Susie and i will be entering third grade.

c. We will be going to the movies on Saturday.

### Capitalization & Punctuation — Answer 1

c.

We will be going to the movies on Saturday.

### Capitalization & Punctuation — Question 2
Which sentence has correct capitalization and/or punctuation?

a. Will you be able to go to the party.

b. The garden was soaked from the rain.

c. Josh is traveling to orlando, florida, for a vacation.

### Capitalization & Punctuation — Answer 2

b.

The garden was soaked from the rain.

### Capitalization & Punctuation — Question 3
Which sentence has correct capitalization and/or punctuation?

a. The infant cried all night long.

b. Did you get to see the game.

c. Monica and jessica both have a dog.

### Capitalization & Punctuation — Answer 3

a.

The infant cried all night long.

# Capitalization & Punctuation
## Quiz-Quiz-Trade

**Instructions:** Cut out each card along the dotted line. Then fold each card in half so the question is on one side and the answer is on the back. Glue or tape the cards together to keep the answers and questions on opposite sides.

---

### Capitalization & Punctuation — Question 4

Which sentence has correct capitalization and/or punctuation?

a. Brent hurt His back last week.

b. The loud firework made me jump?

c. My dance instructor told me I was improving.

### Capitalization & Punctuation — Answer 4

**c.**

My dance instructor told me I was improving.

---

### Capitalization & Punctuation — Question 5

Which sentence has correct capitalization and/or punctuation?

a. Do you enjoy chocolate ice cream?

b. Max forgot his homework on tuesday.

c. How long does this TV program last.

### Capitalization & Punctuation — Answer 5

**a.**

Do you enjoy chocolate ice cream?

---

### Capitalization & Punctuation — Question 6

Which sentence has incorrect capitalization and/or punctuation?

a. Do you study every night?

b. Most students have homework each night.

c. When do you begin studying for a test.

### Capitalization & Punctuation — Answer 6

**c.**

When do you begin studying for a test.

---

*Cooperative Learning & Grammar*
Kagan Publishing • 1 (800) 933-2667 • www.KaganOnline.com

# Capitalization & Punctuation
## Quiz-Quiz-Trade

**Instructions:** Cut out each card along the dotted line. Then fold each card in half so the question is on one side and the answer is on the back. Glue or tape the cards together to keep the answers and questions on opposite sides.

---

**CAPITALIZATION & PUNCTUATION**
Question

**7** Which sentence has incorrect capitalization and/or punctuation?

a. Soccer is a very fun sport.

b. Jesse got a bad grade on her test?

c. My mom bought me a pizza for dinner.

---

**CAPITALIZATION & PUNCTUATION**
Answer

**7**

**b.**

Jesse got a bad grade on her test?

---

**CAPITALIZATION & PUNCTUATION**
Question

**8** Which sentence has incorrect capitalization and/or punctuation?

a. Leslie and Lewis are both wearing braces.

b. I'm getting a dog in june?

c. Please be here at three o'clock.

---

**CAPITALIZATION & PUNCTUATION**
Answer

**8**

**b.**

I'm getting a dog in june?

---

**CAPITALIZATION & PUNCTUATION**
Question

**9** Which sentence has correct capitalization and/or punctuation?

a. Do you like ice cream!

b. I'm buying potato chips today.

c. My brother will want to eat all the snacks?

---

**CAPITALIZATION & PUNCTUATION**
Answer

**9**

**b.**

I'm buying potato chips today.

# Capitalization & Punctuation
## Quiz-Quiz-Trade

**Instructions:** Cut out each card along the dotted line. Then fold each card in half so the question is on one side and the answer is on the back. Glue or tape the cards together to keep the answers and questions on opposite sides.

---

**Capitalization & Punctuation — Question 10**

Which sentence has correct capitalization and/or punctuation?

a. What time will you be home on sunday!

b. officer buckle enjoyed teaching others.

c. Do you like to go to the movies?

**Capitalization & Punctuation — Answer 10**

c.

Do you like to go to the movies?

---

**Capitalization & Punctuation — Question 11**

Which sentence has incorrect capitalization and/or punctuation?

a. Where is your father?

b. I love to eat broccoli for dinner!

c. Please get Out your pencils?

**Capitalization & Punctuation — Answer 11**

c.

Please get Out your pencils?

---

**Capitalization & Punctuation — Question 12**

Which sentence has correct capitalization and/or punctuation?

a. What is your favorite color.

b. Can you take me to the park!

c. What is your name?

**Capitalization & Punctuation — Answer 12**

c.

What is your name?

---

Cooperative Learning & Grammar
Kagan Publishing • 1 (800) 933-2667 • www.KaganOnline.com

# Capitalization & Punctuation
## Quiz-Quiz-Trade

**Instructions:** Cut out each card along the dotted line. Then fold each card in half so the question is on one side and the answer is on the back. Glue or tape the cards together to keep the answers and questions on opposite sides.

---

**Capitalization & Punctuation — Question**

**13.** Which sentence has correct capitalization and/or punctuation?

a. Can we get oranges at the store.

b. I will be 6 years old in December.

c. Wow?

**Capitalization & Punctuation — Answer**

**13.** b.

I will be 6 years old in December.

---

**Capitalization & Punctuation — Question**

**14.** Which sentence has incorrect capitalization and/or punctuation?

a. We traveled to branson this summer.

b. Football is my favorite fall sport.

c. Are you going to Stacey's game?

**Capitalization & Punctuation — Answer**

**14.** a.

We traveled to branson this summer.

---

**Capitalization & Punctuation — Question**

**15.** Which sentence has correct capitalization and/or punctuation?

a. The garbage gets picked up on thursday.

b. Sammy and i received a package.

c. Tommy accidentally threw away his retainer.

**Capitalization & Punctuation — Answer**

**15.** c.

Tommy accidentally threw away his retainer.

---

**Cooperative Learning & Grammar**
Kagan Publishing • 1 (800) 933-2667 • www.KaganOnline.com

# Capitalization & Punctuation
## Quiz-Quiz-Trade

**Instructions:** Cut out each card along the dotted line. Then fold each card in half so the question is on one side and the answer is on the back. Glue or tape the cards together to keep the answers and questions on opposite sides.

---

### Capitalization & Punctuation — Question 16
Which sentence has incorrect capitalization and/or punctuation?
a. Mrs. Brown and mr. John both worked on tuesday.
b. Do you like my pink dress?
c. I do not enjoy going to the dentist.

### Capitalization & Punctuation — Answer 16
**a.**
Mrs. Brown and mr. John both worked on tuesday.

---

### Capitalization & Punctuation — Question 17
Which sentence has correct capitalization and/or punctuation?
a. Sarah found ten Dollars on the ground.
b. How long will the presentation be!
c. Twenty people attended the baseball game.

### Capitalization & Punctuation — Answer 17
**c.**
Twenty people attended the baseball game.

---

### Capitalization & Punctuation — Question 18
Which sentence has incorrect capitalization and/or punctuation?
a. The loud thunderstorm kept Me awake all night?
b. The big tree branch fell on our neighbor's house.
c. I was really scared.

### Capitalization & Punctuation — Answer 18
**a.**
The loud thunderstorm kept Me awake all night?

---

**Cooperative Learning & Grammar**
Kagan Publishing • 1 (800) 933-2667 • www.KaganOnline.com

# Capitalization & Punctuation
## Quiz-Quiz-Trade

**Instructions:** Cut out each card along the dotted line. Then fold each card in half so the question is on one side and the answer is on the back. Glue or tape the cards together to keep the answers and questions on opposite sides.

---

**Capitalization & Punctuation — Question**

**19.** Which sentence has correct capitalization and/or punctuation?

a. Gustav went scuba diving in lake placid.

b. My family has taco night on Wednesdays.

c. The road construction Caused us to be late to our Game?

---

**Capitalization & Punctuation — Answer**

**19.** b.

My family has taco night on Wednesdays.

---

**Capitalization & Punctuation — Question**

**20.** Which sentence has incorrect capitalization and/or punctuation?

a. Swimming is my favorite summer activity.

b. Last november my grandma came to visit.

c. Aliyah will run a marathon on Saturday.

---

**Capitalization & Punctuation — Answer**

**20.** b.

Last november my grandma came to visit.

---

**Capitalization & Punctuation — Question**

**21.** Which sentence has correct capitalization and/or punctuation?

a. The wet dog smelled horrible?

b. Pedro went to paris for a month.

c. The car had a flat tire.

---

**Capitalization & Punctuation — Answer**

**21.** c.

The car had a flat tire.

# Capitalization & Punctuation
## Quiz-Quiz-Trade

**Instructions:** Cut out each card along the dotted line. Then fold each card in half so the question is on one side and the answer is on the back. Glue or tape the cards together to keep the answers and questions on opposite sides.

---

**Capitalization & Punctuation — Question**

**22.** Which sentence has correct capitalization and/or punctuation?

a. President lincoln was an Honest man.

b. The green grass needed to be cut.

c. Jordon and i enjoy reading *boxcar children* books.

---

**Capitalization & Punctuation — Answer**

**22.** **b.**

The green grass needed to be cut.

---

**Capitalization & Punctuation — Question**

**23.** Which sentence has incorrect capitalization and/or punctuation?

a. The computer fit nicely in the case?

b. My birthday party was at Fassnight Park.

c. Your brown hair keeps getting tangled.

---

**Capitalization & Punctuation — Answer**

**23.** **a.**

The computer fit nicely in the case?

---

**Capitalization & Punctuation — Question**

**24.** Which sentence has incorrect capitalization and/or punctuation?

a. Our principal is going to eat three worms.

b. Marcus gave his mother a Bouquet of flowers for mother's day.

c. Uncle Hiroshi brought hot dogs to the party.

---

**Capitalization & Punctuation — Answer**

**24.** **b.**

Marcus gave his mother a Bouquet of flowers for mother's day.

---

*Cooperative Learning & Grammar*
Kagan Publishing • 1 (800) 933-2667 • www.KaganOnline.com

# Grammar Skills 4
# SENTENCES

- **Simple Subject**
  (RallyCoach/Sage-N-Scribe) ...................... 206
- **Simple Subject** (Find Someone Who) .......... 207
- **Simple Predicate**
  (RallyCoach/Sage-N-Scribe) ...................... 208
- **Simple Predicate** (Find Someone Who) ...... 209
- **Complete Subject**
  (RallyCoach/Sage-N-Scribe) ...................... 210
- **Complete Subject**
  (Find Someone Who) ................................. 211
- **Complete Predicate**
  (RallyCoach/Sage-N-Scribe) ...................... 212
- **Complete Predicate** (Find Someone Who) .. 213
- **Subject & Predicate**
  (RallyCoach/Sage-N-Scribe) ...................... 214
- **Complete Subject & Predicate**
  (RallyCoach/Sage-N-Scribe) ...................... 215
- **Subject & Predicate** (Find Someone Who) .. 216
- **Complete Subject & Predicate**
  (Quiz-Quiz-Trade) ............................. 217–224
- **Complete Sentences**
  (Find-N-Fix) ............................................. 225
- **Dependent & Independent Clauses**
  (Find Someone Who) ................................. 226
- **Independent Clauses & Conjunctions**
  (RallyCoach/Sage-N-Scribe) ...................... 227
- **Complete Sentences**
  (Showdown/Fan-N-Pick) ..................... 228–230
- **Combining Sentences**
  (RallyCoach/Sage-N-Scribe) ...................... 231
- **Declarative & Imperative Sentences**
  (RallyCoach/Sage-N-Scribe) ...................... 232
- **Interrogative & Exclamatory Sentences**
  (RallyCoach/Sage-N-Scribe) ...................... 233
- **Types of Sentences**
  (RallyCoach/Sage-N-Scribe) ............... 234–235
- **Types of Sentences**
  (Find Someone Who) ................................. 236
- **Answer Key** ........................................ 251–255

# Simple Subject
## RallyCoach/Sage-N-Scribe

**Instructions:** Take turns working with your partner to underline the simple subject in each sentence using RallyCoach or Sage-N-Scribe.

### Partner A

Name _____

1. My dog chased his ball down the street.
2. The apple fell off the tree after it was ripe.
3. The dolphin jumped through a hoop during the show.
4. The toddler cried after he fell on the concrete.
5. The drama club meets after school.
6. Kevin won the football game after throwing a touchdown.
7. The rocking horse was a present from grandmother.
8. Century Elementary School is presenting a talent show on Friday.
9. The fish jumped out of the water.

### Partner B

Name _____

1. Abdulah was playing on the swings.
2. The crowd cheered loudly during the basketball game.
3. The clowns were making the children laugh.
4. The train is running late.
5. We went on a sailboat during our vacation.
6. Our family is going camping this weekend at the state park.
7. The police officer was helping direct traffic through the intersection.
8. The baby woke up smiling after a long nap.
9. Mr. Martinez is going to the store to buy a new television.

# SIMPLE SUBJECT
## Find Someone Who

Name _____

**Instructions:** Pair up and take turns circling the simple subject of each sentence. Don't forget your partner's initials.

1. Khloe likes to go swimming in Miami.

2. Second grader, Sophia, tap dances during the school's recital.

3. The dalmatian puppy chased the truck down the road.

4. Gavin's teddy bear is missing an eye.

5. The red and white striped ball bounced through the gym.

6. The red fire engine was zooming on the highway.

7. The basketball coach blew the whistle, signaling the end of practice.

8. The boy racers lined up at the starting block.

9. The county hospital is holding a bike-a-thon for area children.

10. My mom baked a three-tiered chocolate cake for my party.

*Cooperative Learning & Grammar*

# Simple Predicate
## RallyCoach/Sage-N-Scribe

**Instructions:** Take turns working with your partner to underline the simple predicate in each sentence using RallyCoach or Sage-N-Scribe.

## Partner A

Name _____

1. The joggers ran down the street during the race.
2. The tree grew three feet since last year.
3. The young boy rode his bicycle down his driveway.
4. Dinosaurs roamed the earth looking for food.
5. The piano makes beautiful music.
6. Kang scrunched up his nose at the bad smell in the trash can.
7. The dancers performed a lovely ballet routine.
8. The giraffe galloped gently across the open savannah.
9. The paint splattered on the floor today.
10. The girls squealed loudly during the sleepover.

## Partner B

Name _____

1. Trevor kicked the winning soccer goal.
2. Butterflies migrate during the cold months of winter.
3. Cedric plays the guitar in a band.
4. Candace writes a story during writing time.
5. The third-graders lined up in the hallway during a fire drill.
6. The bee buzzed over the flower garden.
7. The lava oozed over the volcano.
8. The blue jay chirped peacefully from his nest.
9. The puppy brushed his tail up against my leg.
10. The telephone broke yesterday.

# Simple Predicate
## Find Someone Who

**Name** _____

**Instructions:** Pair up and take turns circling the simple predicate in each sentence. Don't forget to get your partner's initials.

1. The baseball pitcher threw a fast ball over home plate. — Initials

2. A winter's storm left eight inches of snow on the ground. — Initials

3. The children built a sand castle on the water. — Initials

4. Ellie tumbled over the floor mat during gymnastic practice. — Initials

5. Sadiki and his younger brother fished in Lake Erie. — Initials

6. Kyoko typed her report on the home computer. — Initials

7. The green grass turned brown after many months of no rain. — Initials

8. We went to an amusement park for our family reunion. — Initials

9. Otto washed the dishes after dinner. — Initials

10. The starfish hunted for food along the ocean floor. — Initials

# COMPLETE SUBJECT
## RallyCoach/Sage-N-Scribe

**Instructions:** Take turns working with your partner to underline the complete subject in each sentence using RallyCoach or Sage-N-Scribe.

**Partner A**

Name _____

1. The two brothers are best friends.
2. The yellow and blue ball bounced across the court.
3. The giant red strawberry was juicy and sweet to eat.
4. The four library books were delightful to read.
5. The cell phone rang during the movie.
6. The classroom meeting was held to discuss playground rules.
7. The sour lemonade was hard to drink.
8. The loud squealing pig was running loose around the front yard.
9. The dozen chocolate chip cookies were gone before Mom placed them on the table.

**Partner B**

Name _____

1. The salty chips and salsa were a great treat.
2. My older sister and younger brother were happy to go to grandmother's house for the weekend.
3. The three football coaches got together to plan for Saturday's game.
4. The fourth-grade class went to the zoo for a field trip.
5. The steak and mushroom soup was delicious!
6. The Star-Spangled Banner was sung before the volleyball game.
7. Doug and his best friend Brian played video games after school.
8. Drums, guitars, and microphones are needed for the school band.
9. The yellow rubber ducks were left in the swimming pool.

**Name** _____

**Instructions:** Pair up and take turns circling the complete subject of each sentence. Don't forget to get your partner's initials.

1. Ashlyn and Becky ate creamy ice cream for a snack.

2. A little brown puppy wagged its tail excitedly.

3. The roof of the house leaked after the thunder storm.

4. The tricycle's tire needed air.

5. The bright sunshine warmed up the cold ground.

6. The giant oak tree provided shade on a hot day.

7. Our sugar cookies baked to a golden color in the oven.

8. The little red engine chugged up the hilly tracks.

9. The ocean waves broke over the surf.

10. The mountain goat searched for food along the mountain's cliffs.

# Complete Predicate
## RallyCoach/Sage-N-Scribe

**Instructions:** Take turns working with your partner to underline the complete predicate in each sentence using RallyCoach or Sage-N-Scribe.

### Partner A

Name _____

1. My mother cleaned up the living room.
2. The fly landed on my arm.
3. The thirteen puppies chased one another around the park.
4. Grandmother spoke on the phone with her friend Millie.
5. Eugene ate pizza for lunch.
6. The flag flew above the bank on the flagpole.
7. I piled the rocks at the beach into a huge castle.
8. The red and gold scarf blew away in the wind.
9. The sun shines down on the meadow of flowers.

### Partner B

Name _____

1. The horse galloped along the trail.
2. My friends and I played school in my parents' garage.
3. Megan baked blueberry muffins for the school bake sale.
4. The ladybug crawled up the rose stem.
5. Tucker went to summer camp in Wisconsin.
6. The tools in the shed were ruined during the rainstorm.
7. Papa worked in the garden all morning.
8. The ants marched towards the picnic lunch.
9. The girls' softball team won the tournament.

Name _____

**Instructions:** Pair up and take turns circling the complete predicate of each sentence. Don't forget your partner's initials.

1. The iced tea tasted refreshing on the warm summer night.

2. Max and Evan swung on the tire swing in Nana's yard.

3. The fresh flowers grew big in the well tended garden.

4. The crowd cheered loudly for the home baseball team.

5. Jack and Edward completed the jigsaw puzzle during the rainstorm.

6. Maggie and Molly played make-believe with the toy kitchen.

7. The kindergarten teacher helped the class learn to count to 100.

8. The timer beeped when the muffins were finished.

9. The cell phone rang during the movie.

10. The family ate a generous lunch.

# SUBJECT & PREDICATE
## RallyCoach/Sage-N-Scribe

**Instructions:** Take turns with your partner to identify the underlined part of the sentence as simple subject, complete subject, simple predicate, or complete predicate. With your partner solve problems using RallyCoach or Sage-N-Scribe.

## PARTNER A

Name _____

**1.** Neil and his brother <u>visited</u> the museum for a school project.
- a. simple subject
- b. complete subject
- c. simple predicate
- d. complete predicate

**2.** <u>The purple plastic watch</u> tells time under the water.
- a. simple subject
- b. complete subject
- c. simple predicate
- d. complete predicate

**3.** The penguin <u>waddled across the smooth ice</u>.
- a. simple subject
- b. complete subject
- c. simple predicate
- d. complete predicate

## PARTNER B

Name _____

**1.** <u>My favorite yellow shirt</u> tore when I crawled under the wire fence.
- a. simple subject
- b. complete subject
- c. simple predicate
- d. complete predicate

**2.** The young bird <u>tweeted</u> from his spot in the nest.
- a. simple subject
- b. complete subject
- c. simple predicate
- d. complete predicate

**3.** The fast <u>motorcycle</u> zoomed through the race course with ease.
- a. simple subject
- b. complete subject
- c. simple predicate
- d. complete predicate

214 Sentences

*Cooperative Learning & Grammar*
Kagan Publishing • 1 (800) 933-2667 • www.KaganOnline.com

# COMPLETE SUBJECT & PREDICATE
## RallyCoach/Sage-N-Scribe

**Instructions:** Take turns working with your partner to circle the complete subject and underline the complete predicate in each sentence. With your partner solve problems using RallyCoach or Sage-N-Scribe.

### PARTNER A

Name _____

1. My favorite grandmother lives in Anchorage, Alaska.

2. The creamy white chocolate cake was served at the birthday party.

3. Elijah's mom peeled potatoes for tonight's dinner.

4. Carrie, Kanye, and Esteban watched a scary movie at Fred's house.

5. Aleksandra drew a picture of a horse running in a field.

6. Ashley signed up to sing in the school's end-of-the-year talent show.

7. My favorite teacher sang science songs with us.

### PARTNER B

Name _____

1. The raccoon took its family to a new tree to live.

2. The wooden birdhouse hung in the backyard.

3. The winter's storm provided eighteen inches of snow!

4. The white fluffy clouds floated across the bright blue sky.

5. Chai sat down at the piano to play a song.

6. The local newspaper took a picture of my prize pumpkin.

7. Joanna's baby sister collected seashells from the sand.

# SUBJECT & PREDICATE
## Find Someone Who

Name _____

**Instructions:** Pair up and take turns identifying the underlined part of the sentence. Write simple subject, simple predicate, complete subject, or complete predicate in the box provided. Don't forget to get your partner's initials.

| | Sentence | Subject or Predicate (Simple or Complete) | Initials |
|---|---|---|---|
| 1 | <u>Bobby's mom</u> baked sugar cookies for his birthday. | | |
| 2 | Kimmy <u>swam</u> in the ocean during the family vacation. | | |
| 3 | The fifth-grade <u>students</u> put on a play for the school. | | |
| 4 | The city's <u>police officer</u> helped the young boy find his mom. | | |
| 5 | Jenny and her best friend <u>write letters to each other</u>. | | |
| 6 | <u>Our green slimy snake</u> escaped from its cage in the classroom. | | |
| 7 | All the planets in our solar system <u>orbit</u> the sun. | | |
| 8 | The firefighter <u>helped put out the house fire</u>. | | |
| 9 | The house <u>lights</u> flickered during the storm. | | |
| 10 | <u>The blue striped race car</u> came in first at the track. | | |

# Complete Subject & Predicate
## Quiz-Quiz-Trade

**Instructions:** Cut out each card along the dotted line. Then fold each card in half so the question is on one side and the answer is on the back. Glue or tape the cards together to keep the answers and questions on opposite sides.

---

**Complete Subject & Predicate — Question**

**1** Which part of the sentence is underlined?

The remote control <u>fell into the couch cushion</u>.

**Complete Subject & Predicate — Answer**

**1** complete predicate

---

**Complete Subject & Predicate — Question**

**2** What is the complete subject of the sentence below?

Mrs. McKoy took her class to Funland.

**Complete Subject & Predicate — Answer**

**2** Mrs. McKoy

---

**Complete Subject & Predicate — Question**

**3** What is the complete predicate of the sentence below?

The chair fell over and hit the student.

**Complete Subject & Predicate — Answer**

**3** fell over and hit the student

---

*Cooperative Learning & Grammar*
Kagan Publishing • 1 (800) 933-2667 • www.KaganOnline.com

# COMPLETE SUBJECT & PREDICATE
## Quiz-Quiz-Trade

**Instructions:** Cut out each card along the dotted line. Then fold each card in half so the question is on one side and the answer is on the back. Glue or tape the cards together to keep the answers and questions on opposite sides.

---

**COMPLETE SUBJECT & PREDICATE**
Question

**4** What is the complete subject of the sentence below?

The firefighter put out the large house fire.

---

**COMPLETE SUBJECT & PREDICATE**
Answer

**4**

The firefighter

---

**COMPLETE SUBJECT & PREDICATE**
Question

**5** What is the complete predicate of the sentence below?

The clever boy unlocked the kitchen cabinet.

---

**COMPLETE SUBJECT & PREDICATE**
Answer

**5**

unlocked the kitchen cabinet

---

**COMPLETE SUBJECT & PREDICATE**
Question

**6** Which part of the sentence is underlined?

My computer exploded during the storm.

---

**COMPLETE SUBJECT & PREDICATE**
Answer

**6**

complete subject

---

218  Sentences

Cooperative Learning & Grammar
Kagan Publishing • 1 (800) 933-2667 • www.KaganOnline.com

# COMPLETE SUBJECT & PREDICATE
## Quiz-Quiz-Trade

**Instructions:** Cut out each card along the dotted line. Then fold each card in half so the question is on one side and the answer is on the back. Glue or tape the cards together to keep the answers and questions on opposite sides.

---

**7** Which part of the sentence is underlined?

The chef <u>made me a special cake for my birthday</u>.

**7** complete predicate

---

**8** Which part of the sentence is underlined?

<u>The cafeteria ladies</u> serve us a delicious lunch each day.

**8** complete subject

---

**9** Which part of the sentence is underlined?

Today our class <u>measured the length of our books</u>.

**9** complete predicate

---

Cooperative Learning & Grammar
Kagan Publishing • 1 (800) 933-2667 • www.KaganOnline.com

Sentences 219

# COMPLETE SUBJECT & PREDICATE
## Quiz-Quiz-Trade

**Instructions:** Cut out each card along the dotted line. Then fold each card in half so the question is on one side and the answer is on the back. Glue or tape the cards together to keep the answers and questions on opposite sides.

---

**COMPLETE SUBJECT & PREDICATE — Question**

**10.** Which part of the sentence is underlined?

<u>The green snake</u> slithered into the bushes.

---

**COMPLETE SUBJECT & PREDICATE — Answer**

**10.** complete subject

---

**COMPLETE SUBJECT & PREDICATE — Question**

**11.** What is the complete subject of the sentence below?

The dainty teacup fell from the counter and shattered into many pieces.

---

**COMPLETE SUBJECT & PREDICATE — Answer**

**11.** The dainty teacup

---

**COMPLETE SUBJECT & PREDICATE — Question**

**12.** Which part of the sentence below is the complete subject?

The fat dog lay on the couch.

---

**COMPLETE SUBJECT & PREDICATE — Answer**

**12.** The fat dog

# Complete Subject & Predicate
## Quiz-Quiz-Trade

**Instructions:** Cut out each card along the dotted line. Then fold each card in half so the question is on one side and the answer is on the back. Glue or tape the cards together to keep the answers and questions on opposite sides.

### Complete Subject & Predicate — Question

**13.** Which part of the sentence below is the complete subject?

The old man had to use a cane to get around the house.

### Complete Subject & Predicate — Answer

**13.** The old man

### Complete Subject & Predicate — Question

**14.** Which part of the sentence below is the complete subject?

A farmer has to get up very early each morning to tend animals.

### Complete Subject & Predicate — Answer

**14.** A farmer

### Complete Subject & Predicate — Question

**15.** Which part of the sentence below is the complete predicate?

She planted twelve flowers in her garden.

### Complete Subject & Predicate — Answer

**15.** planted twelve flowers in her garden

# COMPLETE SUBJECT & PREDICATE
## Quiz-Quiz-Trade

**Instructions:** Cut out each card along the dotted line. Then fold each card in half so the question is on one side and the answer is on the back. Glue or tape the cards together to keep the answers and questions on opposite sides.

---

**COMPLETE SUBJECT & PREDICATE — Question**

**16** Which part of the sentence below is the **complete** **predicate**?

The lawn chair blew over in the strong wind.

**COMPLETE SUBJECT & PREDICATE — Answer**

**16** blew over in the strong wind

---

**COMPLETE SUBJECT & PREDICATE — Question**

**17** Which part of the sentence below is the **complete** **predicate**?

Mom bought two candy bars at the grocery store.

**COMPLETE SUBJECT & PREDICATE — Answer**

**17** bought two candy bars at the grocery store

---

**COMPLETE SUBJECT & PREDICATE — Question**

**18** Which part of the sentence is underlined?

<u>My mom</u> has to take her dog for a walk each day.

**COMPLETE SUBJECT & PREDICATE — Answer**

**18** complete subject

---

222 Sentences

*Cooperative Learning & Grammar*
Kagan Publishing • 1 (800) 933-2667 • www.KaganOnline.com

# Complete Subject & Predicate
## Quiz-Quiz-Trade

**Instructions:** Cut out each card along the dotted line. Then fold each card in half so the question is on one side and the answer is on the back. Glue or tape the cards together to keep the answers and questions on opposite sides.

---

**Complete Subject & Predicate — Question**

**19.** Which part of the sentence is underlined?

The dentist <u>fixed the little boy's cracked tooth</u>.

---

**Complete Subject & Predicate — Answer**

**19.** complete predicate

---

**Complete Subject & Predicate — Question**

**20.** Which part of the sentence is underlined?

<u>Our fourth graders</u> went on a field trip today.

---

**Complete Subject & Predicate — Answer**

**20.** complete subject

---

**Complete Subject & Predicate — Question**

**21.** Which part of the sentence is underlined?

The remote control <u>fell into the couch cushion</u>.

---

**Complete Subject & Predicate — Answer**

**21.** complete predicate

*Cooperative Learning & Grammar*
Kagan Publishing • 1 (800) 933-2667 • www.KaganOnline.com

# COMPLETE SUBJECT & PREDICATE
## Quiz-Quiz-Trade

**Instructions:** Cut out each card along the dotted line. Then fold each card in half so the question is on one side and the answer is on the back. Glue or tape the cards together to keep the answers and questions on opposite sides.

---

**COMPLETE SUBJECT & PREDICATE** — Question

**22** What is the complete subject of the sentence below?

The infant was crying during the church service.

---

**COMPLETE SUBJECT & PREDICATE** — Answer

**22** The infant

---

**COMPLETE SUBJECT & PREDICATE** — Question

**23** What is the complete predicate of the sentence below?

Maria's family carved two pumpkins.

---

**COMPLETE SUBJECT & PREDICATE** — Answer

**23** carved two pumpkins

---

**COMPLETE SUBJECT & PREDICATE** — Question

**24** What is the complete subject of the sentence below?

The green slimy alien ordered a pepporni pizza with anchovies.

---

**COMPLETE SUBJECT & PREDICATE** — Answer

**24** The green slimy alien

# COMPLETE SENTENCES
## Find-N-Fix

Name _____

**Instructions:** For each set of problems, find the incomplete sentence. Indicate which is incomplete using your Find-N-Fix cards. When your team agrees, fix the incorrect problem by rewriting the sentence in the box.

**1** Which sentence is not a complete thought?

1. Come visit our garden.
2. Put the fruit by the door.
3. Big, beautiful plants.

**2** Which sentence is not a complete thought?

1. Bees are sometimes a problem.
2. Plants can be grown all year long.
3. Many yellow things.

**3** Which sentence is not a complete thought?

1. Plenty of options.
2. Animals enjoy vegetable gardens.
3. Many families live in the north.

**4** Which sentence is not a complete thought?

1. Confident of their hard work.
2. The balloon floated away.
3. They started the project on April 24, 1954.

**5** Which sentence is not a complete thought?

1. The big bug flew in the soup.
2. Tom plays football.
3. Flew 852 feet.

**Cooperative Learning & Grammar**

Sentences **225**

# Dependent & Independent Clauses
## Find Someone Who

Name _____

**Instructions:** Pair up and take turns identifying each clause as dependent or independent. If the clause is dependent, write a D on the line. If the clause is independent, write an I on the line. Don't forget to get your partner's initials.

1. I ran a mile after school
_____ Initials

2. Although I am late
_____ Initials

3. Whenever I am scared
_____ Initials

4. Those rocks are very shiny
_____ Initials

5. Because the dog got out of the fence
_____ Initials

6. Joel ate three bananas
_____ Initials

7. So Polly is a parrot
_____ Initials

8. The game is at noon
_____ Initials

9. Since the milk is gone
_____ Initials

10. Although blue is my favorite color
_____ Initials

11. I don't like ketchup
_____ Initials

12. If we are late
_____ Initials

# Independent Clauses & Conjunctions
## RallyCoach/Sage-N-Scribe

**Instructions:** Take turns working with your partner to circle the conjunctions and underline the independent clauses. Use RallyCoach or Sage-N-Scribe to solve the problems.

## Partner A

Name _____

1. The owl swooped down, but it missed its food.
2. We are going swimming, and I am wearing my new swimsuit.
3. I am very tired, yet I can't put down this thrilling book.
4. My mom loves blueberry pie, so we are going to bake her one tomorrow.
5. You need to clean up your room, or you won't be able to go to the golf tournament.
6. Jasmine was exhausted, but she continued to finish the race.
7. Michael wants to ride the roller coaster, but he isn't tall enough.
8. Jill loves to draw, yet she hasn't finished her project.
9. It is so cold outside, but I love to play in the snow.
10. My Aunt Lissa is coming to visit, and she is bringing my new baby cousin.

## Partner B

Name _____

1. The lion ate all his food, but he still seems to be hungry.
2. My big brother is coming home to visit, and he is bringing me a present!
3. I can't play my video games, for I have not finished my chores.
4. The monkey must be lonely, or he is just very tired.
5. My grandpa use to be an army pilot, so he has some interesting stories to share.
6. I practiced my spelling words, so I got an A on my test.
7. I like to read mystery novels, but I love to write fantasies.
8. Dad said he would be late, but he is bringing us ice cream.
9. The toy rocket launched into the air, but it didn't go very high.
10. The teddy bear was left outside in the rain, so the bear is now soggy and wet.

# COMPLETE SENTENCES
## Showdown/Fan-N-Pick

**Instructions:** Copy one set of cards for each team. Cut out each card along the dotted line. Give each team a set of cards to play Fan-N-Pick or Showdown.

---

### COMPLETE SENTENCES

**1.** Which sentence below is written completely and makes sense?

a. Mom and I went.

b. The large mall is scary.

c. Black tires blown up.

---

### COMPLETE SENTENCES

**2.** Which sentence below is written completely and makes sense?

a. I ran down the street.

b. Big, brown bug.

c. Born in 1980.

---

### COMPLETE SENTENCES

**3.** Which sentence below is written completely and makes sense?

a. While I walked.

b. Pat plays sometimes.

c. Grew green grass.

---

### COMPLETE SENTENCES

**4.** Which sentence below is written completely and makes sense?

a. The black bag.

b. My dog walked.

c. Ran from the rain.

---

### COMPLETE SENTENCES

**5.** Which sentence below is written completely and makes sense?

a. I love to paint.

b. Red paint is.

c. Painted something green.

---

### COMPLETE SENTENCES

**6.** Which sentence below is written completely and makes sense?

a. When time?

b. Why is?

c. Who rang the doorbell?

---

228 Sentences

*Cooperative Learning & Grammar*
Kagan Publishing • 1 (800) 933-2667 • www.KaganOnline.com

# COMPLETE SENTENCES
## Showdown/Fan-N-Pick

**Instructions:** Copy one set of cards for each team. Cut out each card along the dotted line. Give each team a set of cards to play Fan-N-Pick or Showdown.

---

### COMPLETE SENTENCES

**7.** Which sentence below is written completely and makes sense?

a. We swimmed this summer.

b. Lucy is on the swim team.

c. Bright, pink swimsuit.

---

### COMPLETE SENTENCES

**8.** Which sentence below is written completely and makes sense?

a. I runned to the park.

b. Sue needed a blue crayon.

c. Cried did the baby.

---

### COMPLETE SENTENCES

**9.** Which sentence below is written completely and makes sense?

a. The baby fell asleep.

b. Big cry baby.

c. Both baby cry a lot.

---

### COMPLETE SENTENCES

**10.** Which sentence below is written completely and makes sense?

a. School starts Monday.

b. Polka dotted chair.

c. My foots hurt.

---

### COMPLETE SENTENCES

**11.** Which sentence below is written completely and makes sense?

a. Will you please listen to me?

b. You no listen.

c. Don't understand.

---

### COMPLETE SENTENCES

**12.** Which sentence below is written completely and makes sense?

a. And tricks she'll do.

b. Does she do any tricks?

c. My mom and I.

---

*Cooperative Learning & Grammar*

Kagan Publishing • 1 (800) 933-2667 • www.KaganOnline.com

Sentences **229**

**Instructions:** Copy one set of cards for each team. Cut out each card along the dotted line. Give each team a set of cards to play Fan-N-Pick or Showdown.

---

**COMPLETE SENTENCES**

**13** Which sentence below is written completely and makes sense?

a. Carissa walked in the park.

b. The park walked Carissa.

c. Who Carissa?

---

**COMPLETE SENTENCES**

**14** Which sentence below is written completely and makes sense?

a. Teresa could.

b. Pink Princess is she.

c. The tall tree fell down.

---

**COMPLETE SENTENCES**

**15** Which sentence below is written completely and makes sense?

a. Jamie sing last week.

b. Slimy butter on bread.

c. Boys will play each day.

---

**COMPLETE SENTENCES**

**16** Which sentence below is written completely and makes sense?

a. Monsters no scare.

b. What do you want for dinner?

c. We eated a lot of food for breakfast.

---

**COMPLETE SENTENCES**

**17** Which sentence below is written completely and makes sense?

a. Talk you can.

b. Who you no hear?

c. Please listen to your mom.

---

**COMPLETE SENTENCES**

**18** Which sentence below is written completely and makes sense?

a. The good book.

b. Read it I could.

c. Joe reads each day.

# COMBINING SENTENCES
## RallyCoach/Sage-N-Scribe

**Instructions:** In the sentences below, combine each pair of sentences into one. Take turns working with your partner to solve the problems using RallyCoach or Sage-N-Scribe.

### PARTNER A

Name _____

1. Turtles and alligators are reptiles. Turtles and alligators lay eggs.
   _____

2. Moons orbit around planets. Planets orbit around the sun.
   _____

3. A dictionary is an important reference book. A thesaurus is an important reference book.
   _____

4. The mouse was scared. The cat wanted to eat him.
   _____

5. David took out the garbage. Shelly washed the dishes.
   _____

### PARTNER B

Name _____

1. The television is unplugged. The television has not been used for some time.
   _____

2. Angela brought her calculator. Jim brought his calculator.
   _____

3. We found a great parking space. We parked our car there.
   _____

4. The harvest was very good this year. We sold a lot of corn.
   _____

5. It is very cold outside. The kids continue to play in the snow.
   _____

# Declarative & Imperative Sentences
## RallyCoach/Sage-N-Scribe

**Instructions:** Take turns working with your partner to identify the sentence as either imperative or declarative. Circle the correct answer. Use RallyCoach or Sage-N-Scribe to solve the problems.

## Partner A

Name _____

1. Sit down and eat your dinner.
   - Imperative / Declarative

2. The shirt you are wearing today is very pretty.
   - Imperative / Declarative

3. We are going to see a movie on Friday when we go into town.
   - Imperative / Declarative

4. Run over to the market and get some bread.
   - Imperative / Declarative

5. Pick up your shoes and put them in the closet.
   - Imperative / Declarative

6. The rain outside seems like it will never stop.
   - Imperative / Declarative

7. Ginger wanted to write a special letter to our grandmother.
   - Imperative / Declarative

## Partner B

Name _____

1. Janie went to the pet store to buy her dog some food.
   - Imperative / Declarative

2. Answer the door.
   - Imperative / Declarative

3. Watch your little sister so I can make dinner.
   - Imperative / Declarative

4. My favorite present is the one my aunt sent me from California.
   - Imperative / Declarative

5. Please be quiet.
   - Imperative / Declarative

6. Kyle is going to have a sleepover this weekend with his friends.
   - Imperative / Declarative

7. Shawna is going to St. Louis to work in her new store.
   - Imperative / Declarative

# Interrogative & Exclamatory Sentences
## RallyCoach/Sage-N-Scribe

**Instructions:** Take turns working with your partner to identify the sentence as either interrogative or exclamatory. Circle the correct answer. Add the correct end puntucation to complete each sentence. Solve the problems using RallyCoach or Sage-N-Scribe.

## Partner A

Name _____

1. When are we going to visit Papa again __
   - Interrogative / Exclamatory

2. That roller coaster was scary __
   - Interrogative / Exclamatory

3. What do you want to do after dinner tonight __
   - Interrogative / Exclamatory

4. Your grades are fantastic __
   - Interrogative / Exclamatory

5. This surprise party is amazing __
   - Interrogative / Exclamatory

6. Will you be able to go to the store with me __
   - Interrogative / Exclamatory

7. Who is your favorite book character __
   - Interrogative / Exclamatory

## Partner B

Name _____

1. Will you be able to come to my house to study for our science test together __
   - Interrogative / Exclamatory

2. That stage show was really long __
   - Interrogative / Exclamatory

3. The lions at the zoo were humongous __
   - Interrogative / Exclamatory

4. When will we be eating dinner __
   - Interrogative / Exclamatory

5. Come quickly so you don't miss it __
   - Interrogative / Exclamatory

6. Watch out for that red car __
   - Interrogative / Exclamatory

7. I can't wait to go on vacation __
   - Interrogative / Exclamatory

*Cooperative Learning & Grammar*
Kagan Publishing • 1 (800) 933-2667 • www.KaganOnline.com

# Types of Sentences
## RallyCoach/Sage-N-Scribe

**Instructions:** Take turns working with your partner to identify the type of sentences below. Write question, command, exclamation, or statement in the box provided. Add the correct end punctuation to complete the sentence. Use RallyCoach or Sage-N-Scribe to complete the problems.

### Partner A

Name _____

1. Larry wants to go fishing in the morning __
   *Question, Command, Exclamation, or Statement*

2. Where do you think we should go next __
   *Question, Command, Exclamation, or Statement*

3. How much do you think it will cost to buy three teddy bears at the store __
   *Question, Command, Exclamation, or Statement*

4. Clinton plans to ride his bike around the park tomorrow __
   *Question, Command, Exclamation, or Statement*

5. Don't be late for your piano lesson __
   *Question, Command, Exclamation, or Statement*

6. Brr, it's freezing outside __
   *Question, Command, Exclamation, or Statement*

7. Eat your dinner before dessert __
   *Question, Command, Exclamation, or Statement*

### Partner B

Name _____

1. I am so excited for my birthday party __
   *Question, Command, Exclamation, or Statement*

2. My leg hurts __
   *Question, Command, Exclamation, or Statement*

3. My aunt and uncle are coming to visit me __
   *Question, Command, Exclamation, or Statement*

4. I went jogging through the woods __
   *Question, Command, Exclamation, or Statement*

5. Don't run in the hallways __
   *Question, Command, Exclamation, or Statement*

6. Wow that slide is huge __
   *Question, Command, Exclamation, or Statement*

7. Where is the next garage sale going to be __
   *Question, Command, Exclamation, or Statement*

# Types of Sentences
## RallyCoach/Sage-N-Scribe

**Instructions:** Take turns working with your partner to identify the type of sentence as either imperative, declarative, exclamatory or interrogative using RallyCoach or Sage-N-Scribe. Circle the correct answer.

## Partner A

Name _____

**1.** The radio is playing my favorite song.
- a. imperative
- b. declarative
- c. exclamatory
- d. interrogative

**2.** My little brother is playing with his toy train.
- a. imperative
- b. declarative
- c. exclamatory
- d. interrogative

**3.** I got a new puppy!
- a. imperative
- b. declarative
- c. exclamatory
- d. interrogative

**4.** Who are you going to invite to your party?
- a. imperative
- b. declarative
- c. exclamatory
- d. interrogative

## Partner B

Name _____

**1.** Caleb, eat your dinner.
- a. imperative
- b. declarative
- c. exclamatory
- d. interrogative

**2.** The bumper car ride was fun!
- a. imperative
- b. declarative
- c. exclamatory
- d. interrogative

**3.** Kevin is going to run in the race.
- a. imperative
- b. declarative
- c. exclamatory
- d. interrogative

**4.** I can't wait to go to the beach!
- a. imperative
- b. declarative
- c. exclamatory
- d. interrogative

# Types of Sentences
## Find Someone Who

Name _____

**Instructions:** Pair up and take turns identifying the type of sentence as a command, statement, question, or exclamation. Write the answer in the box provided. Don't forget your partner's initials.

| # | Sentence | Command, Statement, Question, or Exclamation | Initials |
|---|---|---|---|
| 1 | Destiny has on a pink shirt today for her class picture. | | |
| 2 | I can't believe I got a new car for my birthday! | | |
| 3 | Please wash your hands before dinner, Megan. | | |
| 4 | When are we going to go to the beach to swim? | | |
| 5 | Chai, what a surprise you have given me! | | |
| 6 | May I please go to the library to find new books? | | |
| 7 | Jacob is excited to be playing football this year. | | |
| 8 | Bobby likes to eat ice cream in the summer. | | |
| 9 | Stop before you get to the end of the street. | | |
| 10 | Turn off the computer so you can do your homework. | | |

**Cooperative Learning & Grammar**
Kagan Publishing • 1 (800) 933-2667 • www.KaganOnline.com

# Answer Key

 **Grammar Skills 1**
ANTONYMS, HOMOGRAPHS,
HOMOPHONES, SYNONYMS ... 238

 **Grammar Skills 3**
PUNCTUATION .................. 247–250

 **Grammar Skills 2**
PARTS OF SPEECH ......... 239–246

 **Grammar Skills 4**
SENTENCES ...................... 251–255

## Grammar Skills 1
# Antonyms, Homographs, Homophones, Synonyms

# Answer Key

### (Page 20) — SYNONYMS & ANTONYMS
*RallyCoach/Sage-N-Scribe*

**Partner A**
1. antonym
2. synonym
3. antonym
4. synonym
5. antonym
6. antonym
7. synonym
8. antonym

**Partner B**
1. antonym
2. antonym
3. antonym
4. synonym
5. synonym
6. antonym
7. synonym
8. antonym

### (Pages 21–23) — SYNONYMS & ANTONYM
*Showdown/Fan-N-Pick*

**Page 21**
1. a. high – low
2. c. sofa – couch
3. b. night – evening
4. a. smart – intelligent
5. b. fat – skinny
6. c. tall – short

**Page 22**
7. b. baby
8. b. pretty
9. a. chat
10. c. repair
11. b. low
12. a. young

**Page 23**
13. c. in
14. a. open – closed
15. b. weep
16. b. laugh – giggle
17. b. slow
18. b. giggle – cry

### (Page 32) — HOMOPHONES
*Find-N-Fix*

1. 1. I ~~scent~~ *sent* the letter to my grandpa in the mail.
2. 3. It is hard to ~~cell~~ *sell* a home without a pool.
3. 2. The brown bear ~~eight~~ *ate* three fish.
4. 1. I ~~red~~ *read* five books over the summer.
5. 1. ~~They're~~ *Their* house used to be painted blue.

### (Page 33) — HOMOPHONES
*RallyCoach/Sage-N-Scribe*

**Partner A**
1. son
2. sale
3. bear
4. witch
5. ate
6. its
7. Oh
8. flower
9. flew
10. plain
11. blew

**Partner B**
1. There
2. scent
3. hole
4. hour
5. board
6. see
7. sell
8. tail
9. two
10. ant
11. deer

### (Page 34) — HOMOGRAPHS
*RallyCoach/Sage-N-Scribe*

**Partner A**
1. b. My uncle gave me a pocket <u>watch</u> for completing my boy scout project.
2. c. My teacher asked me to read to <u>page</u> fifty-six of my reading book.
3. b. I can't wait to <u>play</u> football in the fall.
4. c. The horse <u>bit</u> at the apple because he was hungry.

**Partner B**
1. a. The goat <u>pen</u> had a hole in it.
2. c. My teacher will <u>present</u> a certificate for the cleanest desk.
3. b. Larry, please <u>close</u> your math book.
4. b. The president will <u>address</u> the public in his speech.

### (Page 35) — SYNONYMS, ANTONYMS & HOMONYMS
*Find Someone Who*

Answers may vary.

# Grammar Skills 2
## Parts of Speech

# Answer Key

**(Page 38)**

### VERB TENSE
#### Find Someone Who

1. view – present tense
2. will – future tense
3. call – present tense
4. will – future tense
5. studied – past tense
6. received – past tense
7. will – future tense
8. will – future tense
9. lined – past tense
10. will – future tense

**(Page 39)**

### VERB TENSE
#### Find-N-Fix

1. 1. Mr. Brown ~~run~~ *ran* a 5K marathon.
2. 2. We ~~grown~~ *grew* plants in our garden.
3. 2. We ~~writted~~ *wrote* a book about mammals.
4. 1. It ~~land~~ *landed* over the fence.
5. 3. My dog ~~will~~ jumps 25 inches into the air.

**(Pages 40–42)**

### VERB USAGE
#### Showdown/Fan-N-Pick

**Page 40**
1. kicked
2. ran
3. chopped
4. swimming
5. threw
6. bit

**Page 41**
7. c. jumping
8. c. swam
9. c. walk
10. b. ate
11. c. baking
12. a. caught

**Page 42**
13. noun
14. noun
15. verb
16. verb
17. verb
18. verb

**(Page 43)**

### HELPING VERBS
#### Find Someone Who

1. might
2. can
3. shall
4. has been
5. has
6. will
7. have been
8. should have
9. has been

**(Pages 44–46)**

### HELPING VERBS
#### Showdown/Fan-N-Pick

**Page 44**
1. had
2. will
3. have
4. is
5. am
6. are

**Page 45**
7. was
8. has
9. will
10. can
11. was
12. is

**Page 46**
13. should
14. had
15. must
16. has
17. Has
18. are

**(Page 47)**

### IRREGULAR VERBS
#### RallyCoach/Sage-N-Scribe

**PARTNER A**
1. grown
2. ran
3. ate
4. gave
5. broke
6. swam
7. wrote
8. saw
9. gone
10. came

**PARTNER B**
1. drove
2. threw
3. dove
4. told
5. fell
6. got
7. caught
8. found
9. slept
10. won

# Grammar Skills 2 — Parts of Speech
## Answer Key

**(Page 48) IRREGULAR VERBS**
*Find Someone Who*

1. took
2. went
3. given
4. ate
5. saw
6. took
7. gone
8. came
9. broke

**(Page 49) ACTION VERBS**
*RallyCoach/Sage-N-Scribe*

List of Action Verbs

1. raced
2. washed
4. viewed
6. go
13. worked
17. sang
19. swam
22. roared
23. ate
24. looked
26. divided
27. jumped
28. slipped

**(Page 50) ACTION OR BEING VERBS**
*Find Someone Who*

1. play – action
2. skating – action
3. raced – action
4. is – being
5. was – being
6. watch – action ; takes – action
7. are – being
8. were – being
9. watch – action
10. are – being

**(Page 51) COMPARATIVE & SUPERLATIVE ADJECTIVES**
*RallyCoach/Sage-N-Scribe*

**PARTNER A**
1. tallest
2. tastier
3. hardest
4. biggest
5. older
6. warmest
7. biggest
8. happier
9. long
10. nicest

**PARTNER B**
1. faster
2. coldest
3. sharper
4. nicest
5. slower
6. biggest
7. longest
8. larger
9. fancier
10. fatter

**(Page 52) DESCRIPTIVE ADJECTIVES**
*Find Someone Who*

1. A tornado is a (terrifying) occurrence.
2. A (large) earthquake at sea can generate (giant) waves.
3. (Precious) coral has a (red) color.
4. Animals with shells have lived in the (deep) sea for millions of years.
5. Corals look like (small) flowers.
6. The (small) boat foundered on the (dark) sea.
7. The (back) room was filled with (large, yellow) rain boots.
8. My husband mows an (intricate) pattern into the grass.
9. Sam listened to the (muffled) sounds of his broken radio.
10. The (circle-shaped) balloon floated over the (tall) treetops.

**(Pages 53–55) ADJECTIVES**
*Showdown/Fan-N-Pick*

Page 53
1. black
2. five
3. cold
4. yellow
5. saddest
6. reddest

Page 54
7. a. fatter
8. b. colder
9. c. longer
10. a. tallest
11. b. sweeter
12. b. nicest

Page 55
13. noun
14. noun
15. adjective
16. adjective
17. noun
18. adjective

# Grammar Skills 2
## Parts of Speech
# Answer Key

**(Page 56)**

### ADVERBS
#### RallyCoach/Sage-N-Scribe

**PARTNER A**

Answers may vary.

**PARTNER B**

Answers may vary.

**(Page 57)**

### ADVERBS
#### Find Someone Who

1. carefully
2. crying
3. quickly
4. yesterday
5. under
6. tomorrow
7. noisily
8. generously
9. quietly

**(Pages 58–60)**

### ADVERBS
#### Showdown/Fan-N-Pick

**Page 58**
1. when
2. how
3. how
4. where
5. where
6. when

**Page 59**
7. how
8. how
9. where
10. how
11. where
12. where

**Page 60**
13. where
14. where
15. where
16. when
17. how
18. when

**(Page 61)**

### NOUNS
#### RallyCoach/Sage-N-Scribe

**PARTNER A**

1. dog, rope
2. Michelle, hamburger, Burger Barn, school
3. cow, grass, hours
4. Susan, vacation, week
5. brothers
6. mom, baby, blanket
7. deer, food, meadow
8. Tommy, astronaut
9. Mrs. Barnhart, class, tornados, bottle
10. stop sign, storm

**PARTNER B**

1. bicycle, tree
2. Cameron, mother, day care
3. pillow
4. cars, accident
5. music, concert
6. Jenna, Ana, recital, Saturday
7. Reed, shirt, school
8. police officer, man
9. skunks, places
10. Steven, spaghetti, parents

**(Pages 62–63)**

### NOUNS
#### Find Someone Who

**Page 62**
1. thing
2. thing
3. person
4. place
5. person
6. thing
7. thing
8. person
9. place

**Page 63**
Answers may vary.

**(Pages 68–69)**

### PARTS OF SPEECH
#### RallyCoach/Sage-N-Scribe

**(Page 68)**

**PARTNER A**
1. d. adjective
2. b. verb
3. c. adverb
4. a. noun

**PARTNER B**
1. c. adverb
2. d. adjective
3. a. noun
4. b. verb

---

**(Page 69)**

**PARTNER A**

1. Joe ran up the (red) stairs.
2. Sara was swimming in the (big) pool.
3. Molly saw a (brown) bear in the yard.
4. Anthony walked to the (tiny) store.
5. Audrie washed the (black) dog.
6. Timothy chewed the (disgusting) food.
7. Ms. Kern spoke to the (noisy) class.
8. Levi jumped over the (tall) fence.
9. The tiger licked his (gigantic) teeth.
10. Can you smell the (red) roses?
11. Kylie fell off the (tall) slide.

# Grammar Skills 2
## Parts of Speech

## Answer Key

**(Page 69) cont.**

### Parts of Speech
### RallyCoach/Sage-N-Scribe
### Partner B

1. Jill ran up the (five) steps.
2. The police officer washed the (black) uniform.
3. Jim bought a (pink) pencil.
4. Sandy drove to (sunny) Florida.
5. Tristin borrowed a (purple) crayon.
6. The kids drank (ten) sodas.
7. Ryder hit the (round) baseball.
8. The (green) alligator ran into the lake.
9. The fish ate the (fat) worm.
10. Dad grabbed the (stripped) cat.
11. The (little) girl was crying.

**(Page 70)**

### Parts of Speech
### Find Someone Who

1. adjective
2. verb
3. adverb
4. noun
5. noun
6. noun
7. adverb
8. noun
9. adjective
10. verb

**(Page 78)**

### Plural Nouns: Adding -es or -s
### RallyCoach/Sage-N-Scribe

**Partner A**
1. lunches
2. islands
3. dogs
4. classes
5. works
6. skates
7. helmets
8. brushes
9. branches
10. dashes
11. shirts
12. taxes
13. dresses
14. clubs

**Partner B**
1. crunches
2. horses
3. torches
4. houses
5. foxes
6. blankets
7. boxes
8. hats
9. dishes
10. pouches
11. noses
12. branches
13. nests
14. friends

**(Page 79)**

### Plural Nouns: Adding -es or -s
### Find Someone Who

1. buzzes
2. crashes
3. computers
4. heroes
5. books
6. dishes
7. birds
8. sandwiches
9. cars
10. balloons
11. buses
12. apples

**(Page 80)**

### Plural Nouns: Words Ending in -y
### RallyCoach/Sage-N-Scribe

**Partner A**
1. cherries
2. keys
3. monkeys
4. stories
5. babies
6. ponies
7. strawberries
8. pennies
9. guppies
10. boys
11. chimneys
12. libraries
13. puppies
14. armies

**Partner B**
1. skies
2. supplies
3. parties
4. attorneys
5. valleys
6. companies
7. hobbies
8. donkeys
9. candies
10. days
11. plays
12. pantries
13. berries
14. ways

**(Page 81)**

### Plural Nouns: Words Ending in -y
### Find Someone Who

1. cities
2. pennies
3. keys
4. strawberries
5. turkeys
6. guppies
7. stories
8. ladies
9. toys
10. monkeys
11. chimneys
12. babies

# Grammar Skills 2
## Parts of Speech

# Answer Key

### (Page 82) Plural Nouns: Words Ending in -F or -FE
*RallyCoach/Sage-N-Scribe*

**Partner A**
1. knives
2. roofs
3. calves
4. selves
5. wives
6. leaves
7. lives
8. thieves
9. loaves
10. wolves

**Partner B**
1. beliefs
2. dwarves
3. shelves
4. halves
5. chiefs
6. bluffs
7. safes
8. staffs
9. gulfs
10. briefs

### (Page 83) Plural Nouns: Words Ending in -F or -FE
*Find Someone Who*

1. lives
2. knives
3. wives
4. shelves
5. leaves
6. calves
7. thieves
8. selves
9. wolves
10. loaves
11. dwarves
12. halves

### (Page 84) Irregular Plural Nouns
*RallyCoach/Sage-N-Scribe*

**Partner A**
1. oxen
2. teeth
3. children
4. feet
5. deer
6. octopi
7. sheep
8. buses
9. women
10. bison

**Partner B**
1. mice
2. fish
3. dice
4. attorneys
5. persons
6. men
7. mediums or media
8. swine
9. lice
10. geese

### (Page 85) Irregular Plural Nouns
*Find Someone Who*

1. women
2. feet
3. geese
4. teeth
5. mice
6. children
7. men
8. people
9. fish
10. oxen
11. dice
12. cacti

### (Page 86) Plural Nouns: Review
*Find-N-Fix*

1. 1. ~~wifes~~ wives
2. 2. ~~babys~~ babies
3. 3. ~~shelfs~~ shelves
4. 2. ~~churchs~~ churches
5. 1. ~~butterflys~~ butterflies

### (Page 87) Plural Nouns: Review
*Find Someone Who*

1. sheep
2. days
3. boards
4. passes
5. couches
6. fish
7. lunches
8. mice
9. boxes
10. dresses
11. teeth
12. classes

### (Page 92) Possessive Nouns
*Find-N-Fix*

1. 1. Our family has six ~~dogs'~~ dogs.
2. 2. The ~~childrens'~~ children's hands are very dirty.
3. 3. I found this baseball in ~~Megans~~ Megan's backyard.
4. 1. ~~Arizonas'~~ Arizona's mountains have excellent snow for skiing.
5. 2. Omar pulled back the curtains to let the ~~suns'~~ sun's light into the room.

# Answer Key

**(Page 93)**

### POSSESSIVE NOUNS
RallyCoach/Sage-N-Scribe

**PARTNER A**
1. Matthew's
2. boy's
3. bird's
4. Sara's
5. dog's
6. students'
7. grandma's
8. horse's
9. Billy's
10. baby's

**PARTNER B**
1. girl's
2. pan's
3. Jordon's
4. dog's
5. woman's
6. children's
7. Brady's
8. Robin's
9. cat's
10. boy's

**(Page 94)**

### POSSESSIVE NOUNS
Find Someone Who

1. dog's
2. cats'
3. firefighters'
4. book's
5. snowman's
6. balloon's
7. clown's
8. sister's
9. bears'

**(Page 103)**

### POSSESSIVE PRONOUNS
Find Someone Who

1. my
2. her or his
3. His
4. mine
5. Its
6. My
7. their
8. Our
9. hers

**(Page 104)**

### PRONOUNS
RallyCoach/Sage-N-Scribe

**PARTNER A**
1. us
2. He
3. you
4. me
5. He
6. she
7. They
8. us
9. She
10. theirs

**PARTNER B**
1. Ours
2. Yours
3. We
4. they
5. we
6. it
7. He
8. I
9. her
10. them

**(Pages 105–107)**

### PRONOUNS
Showdown/Fan-N-Pick

**Page 105**
1. You
2. us
3. We
4. I
5. She
6. You

**Page 106**
7. Yours
8. She
9. He
10. Ours
11. you
12. We

**Page 107**
13. you
14. she
15. you
16. He
17. his
18. they

**(Page 115)**

### SUFFIXES
RallyCoach/Sage-N-Scribe

**PARTNER A**
1. wonderful
2. careless
3. baker
4. cheerful
5. worthless
6. reader
7. meaningful

**PARTNER B**
1. gardener
2. successful
3. painter
4. skillful
5. childless
6. jumper
7. clueless

# Grammar Skills 2
## Parts of Speech
## Answer Key

### (Pages 116–117) SUFFIXES & PREFIXES
#### Find Someone Who

**Page 116**
1. **unlock**—undo the lock of
2. **frightful**—full of fright
3. **uncomfortable**—discomfort
4. **painful**—full of pain
   **painless**—without pain
5. **preschool**—before elementary school
6. **reporter**—one who reports
7. **rewind**—wind again
   **unwind**—reverse winding
8. **careless**—not exact or accurate
   **careful**—cautious; exact
9. **colorless**—without color
   **colorful**—full of color

**Page 117**
1. pre(heat)
2. re(wind)
3. (close)ly
4. (beauti)ful
5. micro(phone)
6. (large)st
7. pre(school)
8. (attach)ments
9. (fast)est

### (Page 126) ARTICLES
#### Find-N-Fix

1. 1. Susie chose ~~an~~ *a* piece of apple pie.
2. 2. He was ~~a~~ *an* officer in the Army.
3. 1. Mark has ~~a~~ *an* orange and brown sweater.
4. 1. ~~A~~ *An* honest friend is someone to respect.
5. 3. Carmen thought the car was ~~a~~ *an* ugly color.

### (Page 127) ARTICLES
#### RallyCoach/Sage-N-Scribe

**Partner A**
1. a
2. a
3. an
4. an
5. a
6. a
7. a
8. an
9. an
10. a
11. an

**Partner B**
1. a
2. a
3. an
4. an
5. a
6. an
7. a
8. a
9. an
10. an
11. a

### (Page 128) COMPOUND WORDS
#### RallyCoach/Sage-N-Scribe

**Partner A**
1. -self
2. -man
3. -body
4. -ache
5. -room
6. -day
7. -board

**Partner B**
1. -boat
2. -way
3. -side
4. -book
5. -ball
6. -light
7. -back

### (Page 129) COMPOUND WORDS
#### Find Someone Who

1. a. rainbow
2. b. box
3. c. baseball
4. a. house
5. doghouse, airport, bathroom
6. d. bedtime
7. a. shine
8. a. touchdown
9. snowball, hotdog, strawberry

### (Page 134) CONTRACTIONS
#### Find-N-Fix

1. 1. ~~does'nt~~ *doesn't*
2. 2. ~~wo'nt~~ *won't*
   we'll
3. 3. ~~we'll~~
4. 2. ~~woul'dnt~~ *wouldn't*
5. 1. ~~Iv'e~~ *I've*

# Grammar Skills 2
## Parts of Speech
# Answer Key

## CONTRACTIONS
### RallyCoach/Sage-N-Scribe

**(Pages 135–138)**

**(Page 135)**

**PARTNER A**
1. c. haven't
2. a. aren't
3. b. they're
4. c. didn't

**PARTNER B**
1. d. shouldn't
2. b. He's
3. b. can't
4. a. won't

**(Page 136)**

1. would not
2. they are
3. we have
4. there is
5. he will
6. could not
7. do not
8. does not
9. you have
10. it is
11. should not
12. we are
13. has not

1. that is
2. here is
3. we had/would
4. I have
5. are not
6. we are
7. you have
8. did not
9. has not
10. she is
11. I had/would
12. he had/would
13. were not

**(Page 137)**

1. she's
2. doesn't
3. we'd
4. you've
5. don't
6. they'd
7. weren't
8. that's
9. wouldn't
10. I'm
11. wasn't
12. you'll
13. there's

1. isn't
2. we'll
3. wasn't
4. you're
5. you'd
6. we'll
7. they're
8. I've
9. it's
10. you've
11. aren't
12. he'd
13. she'll

**(Page 138)**

1. she will
2. would not
3. I have
4. you are
5. they have
6. it's
7. what's
8. I'd
9. here's
10. we've

1. did not
2. they are
3. she is
4. they had/would
5. he will
6. who's
7. isn't
8. couldn't
9. I've
10. he's

## CONTRACTIONS
### Find Someone Who

**(Pages 139–140)**

**Page 139**
1. she'll
2. they'll
3. hasn't
4. hadn't
5. we'd
6. it's
7. there's
8. couldn't
9. you'll
10. you're
11. shouldn't
12. weren't

**Page 140**
1. I will
2. will not
3. could not
4. Here is
5. I am
6. we have
7. will not
8. does not
9. she would
10. should not

## PREPOSITIONS
### RallyCoach/Sage-N-Scribe

**(Page 157)**

1. down
2. in
3. no prepositions
4. of
5. to
6. in
7. under
8. until, beyond
9. up
10. for

1. as
2. no prepositions
3. in
4. no prepositions
5. underneath
6. by
7. during
8. through
9. into
10. since

# Grammar Skills 3
## Punctuation
# Answer Key

## (Page 160) CAPITAL LETTERS
### Find-N-Fix

1. 2. My ~~Dog~~ *dog* likes to chase his tail.
2. 1. ~~sue~~ *Sue* enjoyed watching the soccer match.
3. 1. I used to live in ~~st. louis, missouri~~ *St. Louis, Missouri*.
4. 1. Mr. Smith lives on ~~parkdale avenue~~ *Parkdale Avenue*.
5. 2. The ~~Swimming~~ *swimming* pool was 12 feet deep.

## (Page 161–162) CAPITAL LETTERS
### RallyCoach/Sage-N-Scribe

### (Page 161) PARTNER A

1. ~~becky~~ *Becky* and ~~john~~ *John* traveled to ~~new york~~ *New York* with their family for summer vacation.
2. ~~aunt shawna~~ *Aunt Shawna* and ~~uncle kyle~~ *Uncle Kyle* got ~~zooey~~ *Zoey* a teddy bear for her birthday.
3. ~~when~~ *When* will we be able to visit the ~~san diego zoo~~ *San Diego Zoo* in ~~may~~ *May*?

### PARTNER B

1. ~~on monday~~ *On Monday* we will go to ~~dallas, texas~~ *Dallas, Texas*, and on ~~wednesday~~ *Wednesday* we will travel to ~~houston, texas~~ *Houston, Texas*.
2. ~~the vinton~~ *The Vinton* family owns the ice cream store.
3. ~~danielle~~ *Danielle* lives on ~~booneville street~~ *Booneville Street* in ~~kansas city~~ *Kansas City*, ~~missouri~~ *Missouri*, with her sister ~~mary~~ *Mary*.

### (Page 162)

1. a. Jim and dee
2. a. the car is red
3. d. None
4. c. the new York yankees play.

1. b. flag day
2. a. kyle won first
3. b. go to lake pomme de terre
4. d. None

## (Page 163) CAPITAL LETTERS
### Find Someone Who

1. ~~i~~ *I* was born on ~~december~~ *December* 6, in ~~branson~~ *Branson*, Missouri.
2. ~~my~~ *My* sister will go to ~~chicago~~ *Chicago* in ~~july~~ *July* with ~~mr. williams~~ *Mr. Williams*.
3. ~~michelle~~ *Michelle* and ~~i~~ *I* won't be able to attend the party.
4. ~~superfudge~~ *Super-fudge* is my favorite book.
5. Do you think ~~molly's burgers~~ *Molly's Burgers* or ~~frank's taco stand~~ *Frank's Taco Stand* has the best french fries?
6. ~~my~~ *My* dog ~~rocco~~ *Rocco* jumped in the lake.
7. ~~dear grandma~~ *Dear Grandma*,...
8. ~~bill~~ *Bill* and ~~tom~~ *Tom* went to ~~bryant park~~ *Bryant Park* on ~~wednesday~~ *Wednesday*.
9. ~~who~~ *Who* has traveled to the ~~atlantic ocean~~ *Atlantic Ocean*?

## (Pages 164–166) CAPITAL LETTERS
### Showdown/Fan-N-Pick

**Page 164**
1. Snow White
2. John
3. July
4. Alaska
5. Monday
6. I

**Page 165**
7. Minimart
8. Dawson
9. Hunter
10. Who
11. Kingdom Keepers
12. Christmas

**Page 166**
13. a. Wednesday
14. b. Main Street
15. d. None
16. a. I
17. c. Hunter
18. c. Christmas

## (Page 167) CAPITALIZATION OF PROPER NOUNS
### RallyCoach/Sage-N-Scribe

### PARTNER A
1. b. mississippi river
2. d. pizza palace
3. a. branson elementary school
4. c. new england patriots
5. a. mrs. hirahara

### PARTNER B
1. a. flag day
2. b. maria
3. c. ohio
4. a. dr. smith
5. b. wednesday

# Answer Key

**(Page 172)**

**COMMAS**
Find-N-Fix

1. 2. This summer we will be visiting Florida, Alabama, and Kentucky.
2. 3. On July 4, 1776, we claimed our independence from the British.
3. 1. I went to the park with Stacey, Erin, and Sue.
4. 2. Robins can fly, sing, and build nests.
5. 2. Mom fixed peas, corn, and tomatoes for dinner last night.

**(Pages 173–174)**

**COMMAS IN A SERIES, DATES & LOCATION**
RallyCoach/Sage-N-Scribe

**(Page 173)**

**PARTNER A**

1. Jason wanted to take a ball, blanket, and umbrella to the beach.
2. Becky was born on December 3, 1998.
3. Megan, Sara, Jade, and Cassidy wanted to play on the slide during recess.
4. This summer my family is taking a vacation to Baltimore, Maryland.
5. I live at 453 Elm Street in Cleveland, Ohio.
6. On June 28, 2012, we will be going to Orlando, Florida, to visit my grandparents.
7. It rained all day on Wednesday, Thursday, and Friday.
8. My favorite colors are purple, blue, yellow, and white.
9. School started on August 27, 2010.
10. Mrs. Mazen read us a story about a bat, an old woman, and a shoe.

**PARTNER B**

1. Mom gave me a peanut butter sandwich, apple, and juice for my lunch.
2. Mr. Burns was born on September 17, 1983.
3. I have six cats, three dogs, and ten goldfish for pets.
4. Bobby went to the store and bought soda, cookies, crackers, and candy for his campout.
5. Uncle Rusty moved to Mason, Mississippi, for his new job.
6. I got a new bicycle, a bouncy ball, and a harmonica for my birthday.
7. Our cat had her kittens on July 9, 2007.
8. We didn't have school Monday, Tuesday, or Wednesday because of the snow.
9. I needed to pack my toothbrush, washcloth, and shampoo for my trip to grandmother's.
10. Papa and Nana were married June 27, 1970.

**(Page 174)**

**PARTNER A**

1. a. Kolby's birthday was July 16, 2008.
2. a. My family visits Branson, Missouri, every year.
3. c. We need to get eggs, milk, and bread at the market.
4. b. Our plane flew from Denver, Colorado, to Atlanta, Georgia.

**PARTNER B**

1. b. My parents' anniversary was December 26, 1982.
2. a. My favorite colors are purple, pink, and red.
3. c. I was born in New York, New York.
4. c. We will visit my grandma on June 3, 2012, in Orlando, Florida.

# Grammar Skills 3
## Punctuation

# Answer Key

## (Page 175) — COMMAS
### Find Someone Who

1. The four largest countries in the world are Russia, Canada, China, and the United States.
2. The Pilgrims came to Plymouth Rock, Massachusetts.
3. Baseball, soccer, and football are popular high school sports.
4. Washington, Lincoln, Kennedy, and Truman were important presidents.
5. Mercury, Venus, Earth, and Mars are the planets closest to the sun.
6. The Constitution of the United States was adopted on September 17, 1787.
7. President Abraham Lincoln was assassinated on April 14, 1865.
8. The Empire State building is located in New York City, New York.
9. The Pacific, Arctic, Indian, and Atlantic Oceans make up most of the earth's water.
10. My grandma planted lettuce, tomatoes, spinach, and squash in her summer garden.

## (Page 176) — PUNCTUATION
### Find-N-Fix

1. 2. What time is it?
2. 1. Football is my favorite sport.
3. 3. Do you know where the library is?
4. 1. I went on vacation to Florida.
5. 3. Where is the waterfall?

## (Pages 177–179) — PUNCTUATION
### Find Someone Who

**Page 177**
1. ?
2. .
3. !
4. .
5. ?
6. ?
7. !
8. .
9. ?

**Page 178**
1. b. ?
2. c. !
3. a. .
4. a. .
5. b. ?
6. c. !
7. b. ?
8. a. .
9. a. .

**Page 179**
1. c. Maggie is learning to climb the stairs all by herself.
2. a. When will we be going to the library?
3. b. "Mommy, can I have a cheeseburger?" asked Fred.
4. b. At the market we bought apples, bananas, and oranges for our picnic.
5. b. I helped my mom do the laundry.
6. a. That roller coaster was so much fun!

## (Page 184) — USING QUOTATION MARKS
### RallyCoach/Sage-N-Scribe

1. "Turn off the lights," Mother said.
2. Mrs. Gordon asked, "Daniel, are you going with me?"
3. Jennifer replied, "I'd love to come to your party."
4. Anna gave a report called, "Indians of the Northwest."
5. "Are you going to the movies?" Millie asked.
6. The teacher said, "Maggie, you got 100% on your test."
7. José said, "Derek, let's play after school."
8. Luke replied, "It's very cold today."
9. Jessica's short story was titled, "Five Artists."
10. Denzel asked, "Is that a good restaurant?"

1. "Francesca, I'll be home late," said mother.
2. Father said, "I'm going to work."
3. Shimah remarked, "I have finished my homework."
4. Li asked, "How old are you?"
5. "Let's get together next week," said Dina.
6. "Have you read *Charlotte's Web*?" asked our teacher.
7. Vinnie asked, "Where's the car's light?"
8. Aunt Molly said, "I'll be home late tonight."
9. "How much is the toy car?" asked Andrew.
10. "Have you read this poem?"

# Grammar Skills 3
## Punctuation

## Answer Key

### (Page 185) Quotation Marks & Punctuation
*Find Someone Who*

1. Ed said, "let's go to the movies after our club meeting."
2. "When do you want to finish your homework?" asked mom.
3. "I can't wait to go to summer camp," said Susan, "because I will be able to ride a horse."
4. Megan wondered, "I hope to be able to visit my grandmother again."
5. "Mrs. Ipock asked me to take care of the class pet," Jared told his dad.
6. "May I please watch a cartoon?" Chandler asked his older sister.
7. "I hope we will be able to see a shooting star," declared Emma.
8. "I love it when my bare feet feels the cool grass!" squealed Lily to her mom.
9. "May I talk with Mr. Barrnet?" asked the lady on the phone.
10. "Why do butterflies migrate in the winter?" asked a student.

### (Pages 192–193) Capital Letters & Punctuation
*RallyCoach/Sage-N-Scribe*

**Partner A**

(Page 192)
1. My friend, Susan, lives in Baltimore, Maryland.
2. Molly and Maggie like to eat chocolate ice cream at Central Park.
3. Kevin wants to go to Orlando, Florida to swim, fish, and play at the beach.

**Partner B**

1. Patty likes to read mysteries, fairy tales, and fantasy books.
2. When will I be able to return my book to Boone County Library?
3. Ellen went to the Super Eight Movie Theater to watch her favorite film.

(Page 193)
1. c. Tomorrow we are going to the San Diego Zoo.
2. b. I am going to invite Becky, Megan, and Jenny to my birthday party.
3. c. Please pick up your toys before going outside.
4. b. My family is visiting London, England, on March 13.

1. c. Our school band is going to perform at the Greene County Fair.
2. a. I am going to a swimming party on June 5, 2011.
3. c. I play football, soccer, baseball, and golf during the year.
4. a. My sister's dance recital is on Sunday at Central High School.

### (Pages 194–195) Capital Letters & Punctuation
*Find Someone Who*

(Page 194)
1. Where is the dog?
2. The pencil is not sharp.
3. My mom is making pizza for dinner.
4. Stop that runaway cart!
5. My dog loves to chew on its bone.
6. The pizza was yummy!
7. Florida is really nice in the summer.
8. The flower is purple.
9. Which way do I go to the store?
10. Will you help me with this problem?
11. The baby is so cute!
12. When will it be warm outside?

(Page 195)
1. The book, *Charlotte's Web*, is about a spider.
2. It rains a lot in March.
3. It can get very cold in winter.
4. Dr. Seuss was a great children's author.
5. What did you do for Christmas?
6. We are going to the beach this summer.
7. My favorite animal is a dolphin.
8. What will happen if I mix green and yellow paint?
9. My sister went to see Dr. Richmond because she was ill.

# Answer Key

## (Page 206) SIMPLE SUBJECT
*RallyCoach/Sage-N-Scribe*

### PARTNER A

1. My <u>dog</u> chased his ball down the street.
2. The <u>apple</u> fell off the tree after it was ripe.
3. The <u>dolphin</u> jumped through a hoop during the show.
4. The <u>toddler</u> cried after he fell on the concrete.
5. The <u>drama club</u> meets after school.
6. <u>Kevin</u> won the football game after throwing a touchdown.
7. The <u>rocking horse</u> was a present from grandmother.
8. <u>Century Elementary School</u> is presenting a talent show on Friday.
9. The <u>fish</u> jumped out of the water.

### PARTNER B

1. <u>Abdulah</u> was playing on the swings.
2. The <u>crowd</u> cheered loudly during the basketball game.
3. The <u>clowns</u> were making the children laugh.
4. The <u>train</u> is running late.
5. <u>We</u> went on a sailboat during our vacation.
6. Our <u>family</u> is going camping this weekend at the state park.
7. The <u>police officer</u> was helping direct traffic through the intersection.
8. The <u>baby</u> woke up smiling after a long nap.
9. <u>Mr. Martinez</u> is going to the store to buy a new television.

## (Page 207) SIMPLE SUBJECT
*Find Someone Who*

1. (Khloe) likes to go swimming in Miami.
2. Second grader, (Sophia,) tap dances during the school's recital.
3. The dalmatian (puppy) chased the truck down the road.
4. Gavin's (teddy bear) is missing an eye.
5. The red and white striped (ball) bounced through the gym.
6. The red (fire engine) was zooming on the highway.
7. The basketball (coach) blew the whistle, signaling the end of practice.
8. The boy (racers) lined up at the starting block.
9. The county (hospital) is holding a bike-a-thon for area children.
10. My (mom) baked a three-tiered chocolate cake for my party.

## (Page 208) SIMPLE PREDICATE
*RallyCoach/Sage-N-Scribe*

### PARTNER A

1. The joggers <u>ran</u> down the street during the race.
2. The tree <u>grew</u> three feet since last year.
3. The young boy <u>rode</u> his bicycle down his driveway.
4. Dinosaurs <u>roamed</u> the earth looking for food.
5. The piano <u>makes</u> beautiful music.
6. Kang <u>scrunched</u> up his nose at the bad smell in the trash can.
7. The dancers <u>performed</u> a lovely ballet routine.
8. The giraffe <u>galloped</u> gently across the open savannah.
9. The paint <u>splattered</u> on the floor today.
10. The girls <u>squealed</u> loudly during the sleepover.

### PARTNER B

1. Trevor <u>kicked</u> the winning soccer goal.
2. Butterflies <u>migrate</u> during the cold months of winter.
3. Cedric <u>plays</u> the guitar in a band.
4. Candace <u>writes</u> a story during writing time.
5. The third-graders <u>lined</u> up in the hallway during a fire drill.
6. The bee <u>buzzed</u> over the flower garden.
7. The lava <u>oozed</u> over the volcano.
8. The blue jay <u>chirped</u> peacefully from his nest.
9. The puppy <u>brushed</u> his tail up against my leg.
10. The telephone <u>broke</u> yesterday.

## Grammar Skills 4
# SENTENCES

# Answer Key

**(Page 209)**

### SIMPLE PREDICATE
*Find Someone Who*

1. The baseball pitcher (threw) a fast ball over home plate.
2. A winter's storm (left) eight inches of snow on the ground.
3. The children (built) a sand castle on the water.
4. Ellie (tumbled) over the floor mat during gymnastic practice.
5. Sadiki and his younger brother (fished) in Lake Erie.
6. Kyoko (typed) her report on the home computer.
7. The green grass (turned) brown after many months of no rain.
8. We (went) to an amusement park for our family reunion.
9. Otto (washed) the dishes after dinner.
10. The starfish (hunted) for food along the ocean floor.

**(Page 210)**

### COMPLETE SUBJECT
*RallyCoach/Sage-N-Scribe*

**PARTNER A**

1. <u>The two brothers</u> are best friends.
2. <u>The yellow and blue ball</u> bounced across the court.
3. <u>The giant red strawberry</u> was juicy and sweet to eat.
4. <u>The four library books</u> were delightful to read.
5. <u>The cell phone</u> rang during the movie.
6. <u>The classroom meeting</u> was held to discuss playground rules.
7. <u>The sour lemonade</u> was hard to drink.
8. <u>The loud squealing pig</u> was running loose around the front yard.
9. <u>The dozen chocolate chip cookies</u> were gone before Mom placed them on the table.

**PARTNER B**

1. <u>The salty chips and salsa</u> were a great treat.
2. <u>My older sister and younger brother</u> were happy to go to grandmother's house for the weekend.
3. <u>The three football coaches</u> got together to plan for Saturday's game.
4. <u>The fourth-grade class</u> went to the zoo for a field trip.
5. <u>The steak and mushroom soup</u> was delicious!
6. <u>The Star-Spangled Banner</u> was sung before the volleyball game.
7. <u>Doug and his best friend Brian</u> played video games after school.
8. <u>Drums, guitars, and microphones</u> are needed for the school band.
9. <u>The yellow rubber ducks</u> were left in the swimming pool.

**(Page 211)**

### COMPLETE SUBJECT
*Find Someone Who*

1. (Ashlyn and Becky) ate creamy ice cream for a snack.
2. (A little brown puppy) wagged its tail excitedly.
3. (The roof of the house) leaked after the thunder storm.
4. (The tricycle's tire) needed air.
5. (The bright sunshine) warmed up the cold ground.
6. (The giant oak tree) provided shade on a hot day.
7. (Our sugar cookies) baked to a golden color in the oven.
8. (The little red engine) chugged up the hilly tracks.
9. (The ocean waves) broke over the surf.
10. (The mountain goat) searched for food along the mountain's cliffs.

# Answer Key

## (Page 212) COMPLETE PREDICATE
### RallyCoach/Sage-N-Scribe

**PARTNER A**
1. My mother <u>cleaned up the living room</u>
2. The fly <u>landed on my arm</u>
3. The thirteen puppies <u>chased one another around the park</u>
4. Grandmother <u>spoke on the phone with her friend Millie</u>
5. Eugene <u>ate pizza for lunch</u>
6. The flag <u>flew above the bank on the flagpole</u>
7. I <u>piled the rocks at the beach into a huge castle</u>
8. The red and gold scarf <u>blew away in the wind</u>
9. The sun <u>shines on the meadow of flowers</u>

**PARTNER B**
1. The horse <u>galloped along the trail</u>
2. My friends and I <u>played school in my parents' garage</u>
3. Megan <u>baked blueberry muffins for the school bake sale</u>
4. The ladybug <u>crawled up the rose stem</u>
5. Tucker <u>went to summer camp in Wisconsin</u>
6. The tools in the shed <u>were ruined during the rainstorm</u>
7. Papa <u>worked in the garden all morning</u>
8. The ants <u>marched towards the picnic lunch</u>
9. The girls' softball team <u>won the tournament</u>

## (Page 213) COMPLETE PREDICATE
### Find Someone Who

1. The iced tea (tasted refreshing on the warm summer night)
2. Max and Evan (swung on the tire swing in Nana's yard)
3. The fresh flowers (grew big in the well tended garden)
4. The crowd (cheered loudly for the home baseball team)
5. Jack and Edward (completed the jigsaw puzzle during the rainstorm)
6. Maggie and Molly (played make-believe with the toy kitchen)
7. The kindergarten teacher (helped the class learn to count to 100)
8. The timer (beeped when the muffins were finished)
9. The cell phone (rang during the movie)
10. The family (ate a generous lunch)

## (Page 214) SUBJECT & PREDICATE
### RallyCoach/Sage-N-Scribe

**PARTNER A**
1. c. simple precicate
2. b. complete subject
3. d. complete predicate

**PARTNER B**
1. b. complete subject
2. c. simple predicate
3. a. simple subject

## COMPLETE SUBJECT & PREDICATE
### RallyCoach/Sage-N-Scribe

**(Page 215) PARTNER A**
1. (My favorite grandmother) <u>lives in Anchorage, Alaska</u>
2. (The creamy white chocolate cake) <u>was served at the birthday party</u>
3. (Elijah's mom) <u>peeled potatoes for tonight's dinner</u>
4. (Carrie, Kanye, and Esteban) <u>watched a scary movie at Fred's house</u>
5. (Aleksandra) <u>drew a picture of a horse running in a field</u>
6. (Ashley) <u>signed up to sing in the school's end-of-the-year talent show</u>
7. (My favorite teacher) <u>sang science songs with us</u>

**PARTNER B**
1. (The raccoon) <u>took its family to a new tree to live</u>
2. (The wooden birdhouse) <u>hung in the backyard</u>
3. (The winter's storm) <u>provided eighteen inches of snow</u>
4. (The white fluffy clouds) <u>floated across the bright blue sky</u>
5. (Chai) <u>sat down at the piano to play a song</u>
6. (The local newspaper) <u>took a picture of my prize pumpkin</u>
7. (Joanna's baby sister) <u>collected seashells from the sand</u>

## Grammar Skills 4
# SENTENCES

# Answer Key

### (Page 216) — SUBJECT & PREDICATE
*Find Someone Who*

1. complete subject
2. simple predicate
3. simple subject
4. simple subject
5. complete predicate
6. complete subject
7. simple predicate
8. complete predicate
9. simple subject
10. complete subject

### (Page 225) — COMPLETE SENTENCES
*Find-N-Fix*

Answers may vary.

1. 3. Big, beautiful plants.
2. 3. Many yellow things.
3. 1. Plenty of options.
4. 1. Confident of their hard work.
5. 3. Flew 852 feet.

### (Page 226) — DEPENDENT & INDEPENDENT CLAUSES
*Find Someone Who*

1. I
2. D
3. D
4. I
5. D
6. I
7. I
8. I
9. D
10. D
11. I
12. D

### (Page 227) — INDEPENDENT CLAUSES & CONJUNCTIONS
*RallyCoach/Sage-N-Scribe*

**PARTNER A**

1. The owl swooped down, (but) it missed its food.
2. We are going swimming, (and) I am wearing my new swimsuit.
3. I am very tired, (yet) I can't put down this thrilling book.
4. My mom loves blueberry pie, (so) we are going to bake her one tomorrow.
5. You need to clean up your room, (or) you won't be able to go to the golf tournament.
6. Jasmine was exhausted, (but) she continued to finish the race.
7. Michael wants to ride the roller coaster, (but) he isn't tall enough.
8. Jill loves to draw, (yet) she hasn't finished her project.
9. It is so cold outside, (but) I love to play in the snow.
10. My Aunt Lissa is coming to visit, (and) she is bringing my new baby cousin.

**PARTNER B**

1. The lion ate all his food, (but) he still seems to be hungry.
2. My big brother is coming home to visit, (and) he is bringing me a present!
3. I can't play my video games, (for) I have not finished my chores.
4. The monkey must be lonely, (or) he is just very tired.
5. My grandpa use to be an army pilot, (so) he has some interesting stories to share.
6. I practiced my spelling words, (so) I got an A on my test.
7. I like to read mystery novels, (but) I love to write fantasies.
8. Dad said he would be late, (but) he is bringing us ice cream.
9. The toy rocket launched into the air, (but) it didn't go very high.
10. The teddy bear was left outside in the rain, (so) the bear is now soggy and wet.

### (Pages 228–230) — COMPLETE SENTENCES
*Showdown/Fan-N-Pick*

**Page 228**
1. b.
2. a.
3. b.
4. b.
5. a.
6. c.

**Page 229**
7. b.
8. b.
9. a.
10. a.
11. a.
12. b.

**Page 230**
13. a.
14. c.
15. c.
16. b.
17. c.
18. c.

# Answer Key

**(Page 231) COMBINING SENTENCES**
*RallyCoach/Sage-N-Scribe*

**Partner A**
Answers may vary.

**Partner B**
Answers may vary.

**(Page 232) DECLARATIVE & IMPERATIVE SENTENCES**
*RallyCoach/Sage-N-Scribe*

**Partner A**
1. Imperative
2. Declarative
3. Declarative
4. Imperative
5. Imperative
6. Declarative
7. Declarative

**Partner B**
1. Declarative
2. Imperative
3. Imperative
4. Declarative
5. Imperative
6. Declarative
7. Declarative

**(Page 233) INTERROGATIVE & EXCLAMATORY SENTENCES**
*RallyCoach/Sage-N-Scribe*

**Partner A**
1. ? Interrogative
2. ! Exclamatory
3. ? Interrogative
4. ! Exclamatory
5. ! Exclamatory
6. ? Interrogative
7. ? Interrogative

**Partner B**
1. ? Interrogative
2. ! Exclamatory
3. ! Exclamatory
4. ? Interrogative
5. ! Exclamatory
6. ! Exclamatory
7. ! Exclamatory

**(Pages 234–235) TYPES OF SENTENCES**
*RallyCoach/Sage-N-Scribe*

**(Page 234) Partner A**
1. . Statement
2. ? Question
3. ? Question
4. . Statement
5. . Command
6. ! Exclamation
7. . Command

**Partner B**
1. ! Exclamation
2. . Statement
3. . Statement
4. . Statement
5. . Command
6. ! Exclamation
7. ? Question

**(Page 235) Partner A**
1. b. Declarative
2. b. Declarative
3. c. Exclamatory
4. d. Interrogative

**Partner B**
1. a. Imperative
2. c. Exclamatory
3. b. Declarative
4. c. Exclamatory

**(Page 236) TYPES OF SENTENCES**
*Find Someone Who*

1. Statement
2. Exclamation
3. Command
4. Question
5. Exclamation
6. Question
7. Statement
8. Statement
9. Command
10. Command

# Notes

# Notes

# NOTES

# NOTES

# NOTES

# Notes

# Notes

# Kagan
## It's All About Engagement!

**Kagan is the world leader in creating active engagement in the classroom.** Learn how to engage your students and you will boost achievement, prevent discipline problems, and make learning more fun and meaningful. Come join Kagan for a workshop or call Kagan to **set up a workshop for your school or district**. Experience the power of a Kagan workshop. **Experience the engagement!**

**SPECIALIZING IN:**

- ★ Cooperative Learning
- ★ Win-Win Discipline
- ★ Brain-Friendly Teaching
- ★ Multiple Intelligences
- ★ Thinking Skills
- ★ Kagan Coaching

## KAGAN PROFESSIONAL DEVELOPMENT

www.KaganOnline.com ★ 1(800) 266-7576

# Kagan

## It's All About Engagement!

**Kagan is your source for active engagement in the classroom.**

Check out Kagan's line of books, SmartCards, software, electronics, and hands-on learning resources—all designed to boost engagement in your classroom.

**Books**

**SmartCards**

**Spinners**

**Learning Chips**

**Posters**

**Learning Cubes**

## KAGAN PUBLISHING

www.KaganOnline.com ★ 1(800) 933-2667